The Noble Courtship

Rediscovering the Art of Lasting Love

Kobie Malik Muhammad

The Noble Courtship: Rediscovering the Art of Lasting Love is a heartfelt work born from deep reflection, honest conversations, and a sincere desire to explore what makes love last in an age of distractions. It's not a manual but a guide—an invitation to slow down, listen deeply, and rediscover the beauty of intentional connection.

Disclaimer

This book is for informational and inspirational purposes only. It does not replace professional advice or therapy. Relationships are personal and unique—what resonates here may not suit every situation. Please use your judgment and seek expert guidance when needed.

The author and publisher are not liable for outcomes resulting from the use or misuse of the content. Names and identifying details have been changed where appropriate to protect privacy.

Acknowledgment of Boundaries

True love is rooted in honesty, respect, and emotional safety. This book rejects any form of manipulation or harm disguised as romance. Its purpose is to inspire a return to authentic, compassionate courtship.

For permissions, questions, or to connect with the author, please email: [kobiewon@gmail.com], Phone: [317-384-8616]

Thank you for supporting original work and honoring this journey toward lasting love.

With gratitude,

[Kobie Malik Muhammad]

Table of Contents

INTRODUCTION

This book's idea grew from my experience as a parent in a world that moves at a breakneck pace. As parents, we naturally invest our time, energy, and wisdom into guiding our children through life's challenges. Yet, as they mature, our parenting methods must evolve. What worked in their early years may require adjustment or a complete redefinition to meet their changing needs.

Finding the right balance in parenting is both an art and a necessity. If we enforce rules with an approach that is too rigid, we risk pushing our children toward rebellion; a taste of freedom might prompt them to rush unprepared into the world. Conversely, if we allow them too much freedom without guidance or boundaries, we leave them vulnerable to many pitfalls. Parenting is a delicate dance that demands constant adaptation, deep awareness, and a loving heart.

This book is not a foolproof guide, nor does it claim to have all the answers—just as love itself defies a single set of instructions. We live in an ever-changing world where certainty is fleeting. The insights offered here are meant not to replace traditional parenting methods but to provide an alternative perspective that acknowledges the complexity of life and the unique challenges every family face.

Time governs all aspects of life. It moves unceasingly, shaping our past, present, and future. For parents, preparation is our most valuable tool in securing a better tomorrow—for ourselves and our children. In this spirit, this book serves as a form of preparation. It offers single men and women insights that may enhance their future parenting journeys while providing our youth a foundation for building resilient lives.

Healthy individuals are the cornerstone of strong relationships, fostering healthy marriages and stable, loving families. These families form the backbone of thriving communities, ultimately shaping our world's towns, cities, and nations. It all begins with the individual; from that starting point, the ripples of positive change extend outward.

May this book serve as a guide, a source of reassurance, and a beacon of clarity as you navigate the ever-changing journey of parenting and personal growth. Remember that love and preparation are potent forces shaping the future.

PEACE!

CHAPTER ONE

LOVE IS...

When it comes to the most valuable things in life—the treasures we all seek—have you ever noticed the hurdles we must overcome to obtain them? Background checks, credit scores, psychological evaluations, rigorous tests, bank statements, proof of insurance, drug screenings, and even DNA tests are barriers to ensuring that only the most qualified individuals gain access to privileges, possessions, and opportunities. Society demands proof of stability, responsibility, and worth before granting us the keys to homes, careers, and life-changing experiences.

Now, consider diamonds. Extracting a diamond from the earth is a meticulous, grueling process. It begins with exploration and surveying to pinpoint where these hidden gems might lie. Once a promising site is found, mining operations—whether open-pit, underground, or alluvial—commence, requiring years of effort, manpower, and advanced technology. Even then, the diamonds emerge rough and unrefined, needing crushing, processing, sorting, grading, cutting, and polishing to transform them into the breathtaking gems of immense value we admire.

Yet, how much scrutiny do we apply when it comes to our most valuable possession—ourselves? We are beings of strength, talent, and boundless potential. We embody energy, emotion, and intellect, capable of creating, loving, and transforming our world. However, when we give ourselves away—our time, trust, bodies, and love—the criteria often seem minimal. A decent appearance, a car, a job, a home, a sense of humor, and a few enjoyable dates become the checklist. And then, almost without verification, we surrender our hearts.

If diamonds demand a rigorous process to be recognized, refined, and valued, shouldn't we apply the same level of care when determining who is worthy of access to our lives? If material treasures require proof and effort, why do we not hold something as priceless as ourselves to even higher standards?

NOBLE: Having high moral qualities; describing someone as virtuous, honorable, and ethical. In character, "noble" refers to one who demonstrates bravery, generosity, selflessness, and integrity—who does what is right, even in the face of hardship.

The question remains: How did we get here? When did we begin to value material things more than the essence of who we are? At what point did we start playing carelessly with one of the most potent forces known to humanity—love?

Unfortunately, the word and the act of "love" have become commercialized and diluted. Yet love is no ordinary word. It is an energy so universal that no one can escape its influence. The hardened gangster loves; the gentle grandmother loves; even animals express love. The righteous love, and yes, even the wicked love. We all love something—our children, money, land, homes, our faith, fast food, or even the chaos that traps us in cycles of destruction.

But let's return to the heart of the matter. Too often, we enter relationships under the illusion of love, surrendering our best selves—mentally, spiritually, and physically—without first exercising due diligence. We invest our time, emotions, and bodies in someone, believing we are building something real, only to face a painful list of losses and regrets later. Then the truth becomes clear: Love is not a game to be played.

There are many definitions of love. After more than 15 years of marriage—with its ups and downs—I find that the following passage captures its essence perfectly:

1 Corinthians 13:4-8 (KJV)

"Love is patient; love is kind. It does not envy, it does not boast, it is not proud. It does not dishonor others, is not self-seeking, is not easily angered, and keeps no record of wrongs. Love does not delight in evil but rejoices with the truth. It always protects, always trusts, always hopes, and always perseveres. Love never fails."

This book introduces a powerful tool that, when used properly, can transform our approach to relationships. It offers guidance for teenagers, young adults, and mature men and women alike—whether you are in a relationship now or seeking clarity for the future. This tool is called Courtship.

Courtship is not merely dating. It is not a trial-and-error game or a casual exchange of affection without direction. It is an intentional, structured approach to love that prioritizes self-respect, discernment, and long-term commitment. The ideas presented here are meant to shift your mindset and introduce you to a new way of relating to yourself and others.

Warning: This book is for mature audiences only. If you are in "play mode," casually hopping in and out of relationships or entertaining flings without genuine intention, this book is not for you. If you are indecisive, a self-proclaimed player, or unwilling to take accountability for your connections, this book is not for you.

Maturity is not measured solely by age. Some 18-year-olds possess the wisdom of someone twice their age, while some 40-year-olds approach relationships with the recklessness of youth. This book is for those ready—ready to embrace relationships with purpose, understand the actual value of love, and approach male-female connections with the ultimate goal of unity through marriage.

Are you ready?

So, with that being said, let's get started.

Before diving in, I encourage you to approach this information with an open mind and a willingness to grow. As you read, pause if you encounter a word you don't fully understand. Don't skim it over or assume you know its meaning—take a moment to look it up. Truly, clearing a word means more than just reading its definition; it means grasping its full depth, understanding its usage in different contexts, and exploring its synonyms. A single misunderstood word can change the meaning of an entire passage, leading to false conclusions and missed insights.

CHAPTER TWO

CURRENT REALITY

Before we discuss love, relationships, and Courtship, we must first acknowledge where we currently stand. The way relationships function in today's world is shaped by how we define them—and often, we operate on assumptions rather than clarity. To begin, let's break down a few essential terms:

Dating – The act of going out with someone in whom one is romantically or sexually interested. It represents a stage in romantic relationships where two individuals engage in activities together, often with the intention of evaluating each other's suitability as potential long-term partners.

Girlfriend – A female partner with whom a man or boy is romantically or sexually involved, reflecting a modern construct that can sometimes be defined by fleeting labels or transient interactions.

Boyfriend – A male partner with whom a woman or girl is romantically or sexually involved, a role that too often is defined by societal expectations rather than genuine connection.

Romantic – Relating to or characteristic of romance; suggestive of idealized love and deep emotional connection.

Imbued with idealism, a desire for adventure, chivalry, and passion.

Characterized by a preoccupation with love or the idealization of what love should be.

At first glance, these definitions might appear straightforward, yet upon closer examination, they reveal much about how we frame relationships in modern society. The central question arises: Are these definitions enough? Do they truly guide us toward meaningful, lasting connections, or do they inadvertently set us up for confusion and disappointment?

In the next section, we will explore how these words shape our understanding of love and relationships and examine whether they align with the deeper purpose of Courtship.

Does Monogamous Dating Even Exist Anymore?

With the rise of social media and constant connectivity, meeting new people has become as simple as pushing a button. The term "dating" has morphed into something so loosely defined that it now carries multiple meanings, varying dramatically from one person to the next. What once implied intentional commitment has transformed into a broad, often casual exchange of time, emotions, and intimacy—sometimes without any clear direction or purpose.

One might argue that modern dating has become an enemy of any strong community. Why? Because in most cases, dating is not just about getting to know someone; it involves an intricate "exchange" of time, finances, DNA, emotions, energies, and spiritual connections. And when a relationship ends, these exchanges don't simply vanish. Instead, they linger, consciously or subconsciously, into the next relationship, the next partner, or even the following environment. Over time, this relentless cycle of attachments and breakups leaves many at a breaking point where they finally cry, "I'm tired of the games. I want to find that one person and settle down." Yet, the emotional and practical damage has already been done by then.

Fast forward to marriage. After years of casual dating, broken connections, and accumulated emotional baggage, two people unite. Yet, six months into the marriage, they may be trapped in a conflict storm. Why? Because they unknowingly brought with them remnants of past relationships—financial burdens, emotional wounds, mental struggles, and spiritual imprints from previous partners. When you add children into the mix, the blessings and chaos multiply, and what was meant to be a sacred union transforms into a battleground where past traumas clash under one roof.

Modern dating, in its current form, stealthily undermines the foundation of stable relationships. It replaces meaningful, enduring connections with cycles of temporary pleasure and long-term pain.

The Modern Dating Landscape: A Game No One Wins

Today's world has normalized a reality where the hidden costs of casual relationships are rarely acknowledged until the damage is already done. People give themselves away without fully understanding that every exchange of time, emotion, and energy comes with a price—sometimes immediate, sometimes far down the road.

Let's be candid: a significant amount of playing is involved from both men and women. Social media has transformed relationships into entertainment, often glorifying dysfunction in pursuit of likes and subscribers. Debates over gender roles, man-versus-woman conflicts, and toxic narratives flood the media. One must ask, however, what the true purpose behind these dynamics is. Is it a genuine concern for love and unity or another strategy to keep people divided and emotionally distracted?

Many protect their hearts not by nurturing them with care but by avoiding commitment altogether. It's as if maturity—accurate self-awareness and emotional intelligence—has been misinterpreted as a weakness. Instead of approaching relationships with sincerity and intention, many engage in a game of "You go first," waiting for the other person to prove their love before entirely investing. Yet, beneath all the games, our shared humanity remains. We yearn for companionship, security, and something real—love, loyalty, and intimacy—without necessarily wanting to bear the accountability and structure that come with genuine commitment.

After all the playing, casual exchanges, and temporary thrills, the inevitable result is heartbreak and a profound loss.

However, if you are currently in a girlfriend-boyfriend relationship, know this book is not meant to cast a shadow over your situation. On the contrary, it is encouraging that you are open to these insights and are willing to grow. The goal here is not to criticize but to empower you on your journey. The steps outlined in this book will help you better yourself and guide you toward the ultimate goal of marriage—building a solid foundation for a lasting, meaningful relationship.

What About Our Youth?

If this is the reality of relationships today, imagine what our children are growing up witnessing. They are entering a world where:

- ❖ Peer pressure is overwhelming.
- ❖ Self-image issues are at an all-time high.
- ❖ Anxiety and depression are rampant

The very concept of love is distorted before they even experience it.

If nothing else, this book is for them. We have an opportunity—and a responsibility—to help the next generation avoid the heartbreak, confusion, and wasted time so many have endured. As parents, we cannot merely hope that our teenagers will meet the right person when the time comes. Hope, after all, is not a strategy. We must equip them with actual knowledge, practical guidance, and tangible tools to navigate relationships with wisdom and purpose.

Some of our youth will listen; some may not. But our duty remains to provide them with something substantial—a lifeline of clarity and direction.

A Question Worth Asking…

Why did God allow puberty to precede maturity? Consider this: Why are young people physically capable of reproduction long before they are mentally or emotionally ready for the responsibilities of adult relationships? Part of the answer lies in history. In the past, there was a robust family structure and a profound sense of community when puberty arrived. Elders actively guided the youth through this critical phase of life. Ceremonies, rites of passage, and structured teachings prepared young men and women for adulthood. They were not left to navigate these complexities alone, nor were they misled by media or societal trends. Instead, they received the structure, wisdom, and clear guidance necessary to assume their roles as mature individuals.

Somewhere along the line, that structure was lost, and now we are witnessing the consequences. It is time to restore that sense of purpose and direction—not just for ourselves but for future generations.

This book is not solely about relationships but about restoring clarity in a world filled with confusion. It is about helping individuals recognize their intrinsic worth before giving themselves away too quickly. It is about breaking cycles of emotional baggage and rebuilding strong foundations for love, family, and community. Keep reading if you are ready to shift your mindset and approach relationships with renewed purpose. What you do not know can hurt you, while the knowledge you choose to embrace can change your future.

A Return to Responsibility

Throughout history, entering into relationships has come with inherent training and a sense of responsibility. A mindset was cultivated to help manage our natural urges and emotions. While those urges are undeniably strong, the presence of a solid family unit, a supportive community, and clear guidance helped individuals maintain control over their lives.

This book is a small part of the effort to revive those values. Imagine a world where our loved ones are spared the deep losses that stem from reckless relationships—a world where meeting the one does not come with the heavy baggage of past failures. Imagine finding that special person with few or no past entanglements, free from the scars of heartbreak, mistrust, or resentment.

That, ultimately, is the power of Courtship.

CHAPTER THREE

THE WHAT? OF COURTSHIP

Before we embark on this journey, I want to put forth this important disclaimer. The effectiveness of this book, the courtship process itself, and the wisdom found within these guidelines depend entirely on how well you understand and appreciate the principles of Courtship. How you value yourself—and the process—will ultimately determine the success of what you gain from this knowledge. This information is not for you if you consider yourself too grown or enjoy bending the rules. Courtship demands discipline, self-awareness, and a willingness to follow time-tested principles designed for your benefit.

Too often, we claim we are courting when, in truth, we are simultaneously pursuing our desires, mixing personal inclinations with a structured process meant to guide us. In doing so, we may marry someone while believing we got away with certain choices or behaviors—only to later pay the price for those actions. We frequently fail to realize that every action has consequences, even if they aren't immediately apparent. Effects may not manifest during dating or engagement but might emerge months or years after the vows have been exchanged. When these consequences eventually surface, they catch us off guard, leaving us to wonder how everything unraveled when, in reality, the foundation was never correctly laid.

Many who declare, "Don't get married," or who look down on marriage, often speak from a place shaped by their own experiences with broken relationships, failed unions, or a misunderstanding of what marriage indeed demands. Usually, these individuals have never been married or have experienced marriages that began on unstable ground— marriages in which physical and emotional boundaries were blurred without a proper understanding of one another. Rushing into marriage without discipline, patience, and adequate discernment only paves the way for disillusionment, leading many to question the institution of marriage rather than reflecting on their choices beforehand.

So please take the time to delve into the wisdom of these guidelines. Study what it means to be disciplined. Learn how to be content and whole while solo during this phase of your life to gain clarity and see your future with a clear mind and a pure heart. Courtship is not just about finding a partner; it's about becoming a person who is genuinely ready for the commitment, responsibility, and abundant blessings that marriage brings. It's about looking beyond the superficial and, ensuring that you are on the right path and journeying with the right person.

KEYWORDS: "KNOW" and "PRIOR"

Know: To be aware of something through observation, inquiry, or information; to be confident or sure.

Absolutely: Used to emphasize a strong or exaggerated statement.

Prior: Coming before in time, order, or importance.

LOL (List of Losses) represents the cumulative adverse outcomes, such as poor credit, mental abuse, broken hearts, death, mistrust, resentment, regret, etc.

In short, that is what Courtship is all about. It is the opportunity to know before you exchange—to gain clarity before you invest your emotions, time, energy, and ultimately your future in another person. It is a safeguard, a tangible form of wisdom in action, ensuring that both parties are prepared for commitment and fully transparent about who they are. This process requires both individuals to be mature enough not to hide anything, deceive, manipulate, and certainly not play games with each other's hearts, time, or destiny.

Once again, Courtship is intended for mature audiences only. It is not meant for those who still cling to a childish mindset regarding relationships, for those who believe shortcuts or avoiding accountability will suffice, or for those who operate based on temporary emotions rather than seeking a long-term commitment. If you encounter someone who dismissively declares, "I'm too grown for this," or "I'm not doing courtship," or even laughs it off as a joke, take that as an immediate signal to move on. Please do not waste your time trying to convince them otherwise, do not engage in fruitless arguments, and do not feel obligated to explain your position. Recognize that such individuals are not ready for anything serious—and that is perfectly acceptable.

There is no need to feel frustrated, disappointed, or discouraged. Instead, be grateful for their honesty. Thank them for revealing their mindset upfront. Thank God for allowing you to see their perspective before you become too emotionally invested. That moment of clarity, whether intentional or not, is a blessing in disguise—it saves you from wasting your precious time with someone who was never meant for you. Every moment saved by walking away from the wrong person is preserved for the right one. Courtship is about moving forward with wisdom, discernment, and clarity. So when someone reveals that they are not aligned with these values, see it as a sign and keep moving with confidence and peace.

Additional Key Definitions:

What: Asking for information or specifying something to find out or discover.

Circumstances: The facts or conditions connected with or relevant to an event or action; they also refer to one's spiritual, mental, or physical welfare.

Guidelines: General rules, principles, or advice that create a framework for behavior without prescribing exact actions.

Wisdom: The quality of having experience, knowledge, and good judgment; the soundness of an action or decision in light of experience and insight.

Discipline: The process of training or developing oneself within a set of guidelines and principles, particularly about self-control.

What is Courtship?

To offer an analogy, imagine Courtship as the security straps and buckles on a roller coaster of life. It is a safeguard—necessary protection to ensure that when you embark on the unpredictable ride of relationships, you remain securely fastened against the forces of unchecked emotion, impulsive decisions, or misguided attractions. Life presents countless opportunities to meet new people—whether at the workplace, in college, during social gatherings, or simply through daily encounters. The thrill of connection, attraction, and companionship can be compared to the excitement of boarding a roller coaster, where you anticipate the highs and lows, the twists and turns, and the exhilarating rush of something new. However, if you're not securely strapped in, the ride can quickly turn dangerous—even disastrous.

Courtship functions as those essential security straps. It ensures that as you explore and get to know someone, you do so in a manner that safeguards you emotionally, mentally, spiritually, and even physically. While your intent might be to have fun and explore possibilities, without the discipline, structure, and security provided by Courtship, what should be an enjoyable journey can quickly become a path to destruction.

Courtship is a designated period during which two individuals can truly understand one another without the distractions, pressures, and emotional entanglements often accompanying modern dating. It is an intentional, structured process that typically lasts between six months to one year—though this can vary based on circumstances and, most importantly, the maturity of both individuals. This is not a casual dating scenario driven solely by emotions; it is a period defined by clear boundaries. These boundaries ensure that both parties understand each other's character, values, beliefs, and long-term goals before making significant commitments. For example, there is no physical touching allowed during this period, as physical intimacy can cloud judgment and create misleading connections that overstate compatibility. Courtship includes chaperoned dates to maintain accountability in interactions, ensuring that both parties engage in meaningful conversation and shared activities rather than being consumed solely by physical attraction. It even includes ending communication by 11 p.m. because late-night discussions often lead to emotional vulnerabilities or inappropriate exchanges.

I understand that this approach is quite contrary to the norms we have grown accustomed to. It challenges what society has conditioned us to accept as usual in relationships. Even as we age—in our 20s, 30s, or 40s—we often adopt the mindset, "I'm too grown for that childish stuff." Yet, the real question we must ask is: where has this "grown" mentality honestly gotten us? If doing things our way on our terms has genuinely worked, why do so many relationships and marriages fail? Why do countless individuals find themselves heartbroken, confused, and emotionally drained? Why is there a recurring pattern of broken relationships, failed commitments, and cycles of disappointment? If the modern approach to dating has resulted in so many painful outcomes, perhaps it is time to consider that the guidelines of Courtship—restrictive though they may seem—are precisely what can lead to real, lasting love. Love is built on a solid foundation of security and true understanding rather than on impulse, fleeting emotion, or superficial attraction.

Six Months to One Year: A Structured Window of Time

The six-month to one-year timeframe is not etched in stone, nor is there any moral authority dictating that it must be precisely that short or long. Instead, this period serves as a guideline—a structured window of time that allows two individuals to honestly assess one another before committing to marriage. Each couple's unique circumstances play a significant role in determining the appropriate length of Courtship. Factors such as physical distance, personal maturity, individual readiness, and clarity regarding each person's desires contribute to the process. Every relationship is different; while some couples may require additional time to evaluate compatibility fully, others might reach a meaningful decision more quickly.

However, committing to at least six months is highly recommended as a general rule. Jumping into a relationship too quickly—without proper evaluation, emotional discipline, and clear communication—often leads to adverse outcomes. Rushing the process can cause people to overlook red flags, misinterpret compatibility, or become swept up in emotions without genuinely understanding the person they are considering for a lifelong commitment. Conversely, the courtship process should not be dragged out indefinitely. There is a delicate balance between taking the necessary time to make a sound decision and allowing indecision to stall progress. No one enjoys dealing with perpetual uncertainty, hesitation, or an inability to decide what one wants. Indecisiveness in Courtship is a major red flag. If, after six months to a year of structured interaction—answering courtship questions, engaging in chaperoned dates, and following all the necessary procedures—a person still does not know what they want, it is time to move on. There is no need to force clarity where it does not exist or to linger with someone incapable of making a decision.

The beauty of Courtship lies in its design: since no premature physical, emotional, or financial exchanges have been made, there should be no deep heartbreak or lingering pain when one chooses to walk away. The structure of Courtship protects both individuals from unnecessary entanglements that can lead to devastating consequences. During this period, avoiding getting caught up in superficial attractions or emotional fluff is essential. Keeping emotions in check and approaching the process with a clear mind and logical thinking are critical. The goal is to see each other as we are, not through the distorted lens of temporary infatuation or excitement.

This structured process does not mean Courtship should be dull, rigid, or lifeless. Laughter, joy, and fun are essential to any healthy relationship and will be even more critical in marriage. Learning how to enjoy one another's company respectfully and meaningfully is just as important as assessing long-term compatibility and goals. There must be a balance between taking the process seriously and allowing room for natural connection and enjoyment. Respecting your own time and that of your partner ensures that the Courtship is purposeful, intentional, and ultimately beneficial—whether it culminates in marriage or the mutual decision to part ways.

No Physical Touch: A Safeguard for Clarity

There is a wealth of science regarding the human touch—its power to connect us, influence our emotions, and even alter our brain chemistry. Studies in neuroscience have demonstrated that physical touch releases oxytocin, often called the "bonding hormone" or "love hormone," which creates feelings of closeness, attachment, and trust. Alongside oxytocin, dopamine (the pleasure chemical) and serotonin (a key mood regulator) are also released, intensifying emotions and often leading to a state of euphoria in the presence of another person. However, these chemical reactions do not necessarily indicate true compatibility, shared values, or a deep understanding of the person before you. They can cloud judgment and make it difficult to notice any underlying flaws, inconsistencies, or red flags.

In the context of Courtship, physical touch is a slippery slope. When the person you are getting to know says all the right things, makes you laugh, looks good, and even smells appealing, it becomes easy to rationalize small gestures— holding hands, sharing a hug, or an arm around the back. Yet, these seemingly innocent actions can spark robust emotional and physiological responses that lead to progressively more significant steps: from a quick touch to a lingering embrace, to a kiss, and eventually to more intimate contact. Each step has the potential to blur boundaries, and before you know it, what began as a cautious exploration turns into a cascade of intimacy that may not be built on a solid foundation.

The consequence of introducing physical intimacy too early is significant. The human body is wired to chase pleasure, yet that same pleasure can deceive us. Once physical interaction enters the picture, our ability to maintain a logical, reasonable perspective diminishes. Research shows that as sexual attraction and physical interaction intensify, the prefrontal cortex—responsible for rational thinking, decision-making, and impulse control—tends to recede into the background. Instead, the emotional and pleasure centers dominate, making it more likely that red flags will be overlooked, toxic behaviors excused, and a relationship mistakenly validated simply because it "feels good" at the moment.

In the Holy Qur'an, Allah (God) advises, "Do not go near fornication or adultery." This commandment warns against the act itself but against even the subtle actions that lead toward it. The wisdom behind this is clear: avoiding the small, seemingly harmless steps prevents the more enormous mistakes from ever occurring. Once a person starts moving in that direction, it is tough to reverse course. This is why I adhere to a strict principle: no private physical exchanges during the courtship period. This guideline serves as a safeguard—a measure of protection that ensures self-control remains intact and that the focus of Courtship stays on truly understanding the person's values, character, and readiness for a lifelong partnership.

An added benefit of this approach is that if the Courtship does not lead to a lasting connection, both parties can walk away without the burden of emotional damage associated with premature physical intimacy. There is no lingering sense of being used or betrayed—only the clarity that comes from an untainted process. The purity of this method allows each individual to move forward without the baggage that often comes with early physical involvement, thereby making it easier to recognize and accept when someone is not the right match.

Chaperoned Dates

I know it might sound a bit corny at first, but we must ask ourselves: what type of results are we truly achieving with our current practices? If modern dating were truly effective in fostering solid, long-lasting relationships—ones built on trust, commitment, and genuine compatibility—then perhaps we could dismiss the concept of chaperoned dates as outdated. However, the reality is that too many relationships today are founded on surface-level attraction, instant gratification, and a lack of accountability. These shortcomings often lead to heartbreak, confusion, and the accumulation of emotional baggage.

Chaperoned dates are not meant to be suffocating, restrictive, or juvenile. Instead, they serve as a structured safeguard designed to maintain respect, discipline, and purpose throughout the courtship process. The presence of a chaperone is not about hovering over every move or micromanaging conversation. Rather, it is a subtle reminder of the guidelines that both parties have agreed to follow. A chaperone might be seated a few tables away, blending naturally into the background, yet their mere presence serves as a constant indicator that the interaction is being held to a higher standard.

The Role of the Chaperone

During these dates, having a responsible couple or individual in the background is immensely helpful. They act as an extra set of eyes, ensuring that both individuals conduct themselves with dignity, self-control, and respect. Their role extends beyond mere supervision. At times, a chaperone may ask questions that are difficult for the couple to broach on their own—questions that are essential for uncovering deeper values, clarifying intentions, and identifying potential red flags. This input is invaluable, as emotional involvement can sometimes obscure objective judgment.

A chaperone's observations can reveal subtle details that might otherwise go unnoticed. Whether it's a particular attitude, an offhand remark, or even the way someone reacts under mild pressure, these insights can help both parties—and sometimes even the chaperone—recognize signs of incompatibility or deeper issues. Importantly, the chaperone is not there to judge or interfere but to support the integrity of the process, ensuring that no one is blinded by temporary emotions or superficial charm.

Maintaining Boundaries and Preventing Temptation

Another critical aspect of chaperoned dates is the prevention of behaviors that might derail the courtship process. The presence of a chaperone discourages any attempts to sneak away or engage in physical intimacy that is not in keeping with the agreed guidelines. This measure isn't about distrust; it's about recognizing the powerful pull of human nature.

Even the most well-intentioned individuals can be tempted to bypass established boundaries when emotions run high. The chaperone serves as a tangible reminder to stay on course, thereby reducing the risk of impulsive decisions that could lead to long-term complications.

In this context, chaperoned dates are not merely about adherence to rules—they are about creating an environment conducive to genuine connection. They help both individuals remain focused on meaningful conversation and mutual understanding rather than being swept away by the initial thrill of physical attraction.

Selecting the Right Chaperone

Finding a suitable chaperone can be challenging, but it is crucial for the success of the courtship process. Ideally, a married couple—preferably related to one or both of the courting individuals—would serve as the best option. If that is not possible, then a married couple from the spiritual or believing community, who share the same values and principles, is a strong alternative. Should neither option be available, a relative (such as an aunt, uncle, or parent) may be appropriate, or even a sincere, trustworthy friend who understands and respects the purpose of Courtship.

Financial and Behavioral Insights

Chaperoned dates can also provide subtle insights into the financial attitudes and overall responsibility of those involved. Traditionally, the expectation is that the male should cover all expenses unless the chaperones indicate otherwise. This practice is not about enforcing outdated gender roles but about emphasizing responsibility, provision, and thoughtfulness. For instance, if a young man hesitates to take on the full responsibility of the date or seems unwilling to acknowledge the role of the chaperones, it might signal deeper issues related to accountability or maturity. Similarly, if a young woman displays behavior that suggests entitlement or a lack of financial awareness, these small details may point to larger compatibility challenges.

In essence, the role of a chaperone is not simply to supervise but to foster an environment where both individuals can display proper behavior with clear intent. The goal is to build a strong foundation rooted in discipline, wisdom, and mutual respect. The chaperone's presence reinforces that the process is not about following arbitrary rules but about ensuring that both parties are genuinely aligned and prepared for a meaningful, long-term commitment.

While this structured approach might feel foreign compared to modern dating practices, when measured against the backdrop of broken relationships, heartbreaks, and lingering emotional wounds, it becomes evident that an intentional and safeguarded approach to Courtship can lead to more fulfilling and lasting connections.

Late-night FaceTime and Conversations are Highly Discouraged

This guideline may turn many people away at first glance. Restricting late-night conversations, FaceTime calls, texting, and direct messages might seem unnecessary, but a closer look at the psychology and science behind it makes the reasoning clear. As the night progresses, our communication naturally shifts. Conversations that begin logical, focused, and intentional earlier in the day often become less structured and more emotionally driven as the night wears on.

The Science Behind Late-Night Communication

It is not mere speculation—this phenomenon is backed by research in psychology and neuroscience. As we grow tired, our cognitive functions decline, and impulse control weakens. The prefrontal cortex—the area responsible for rational thinking, decision-making, and self-regulation—begins to slow down. Simultaneously, the limbic system, which governs emotions and desires, takes over. This shift means that people tend to say and do things at night that they might otherwise avoid during the day. What starts as a clear, purposeful conversation can devolve into one filled with emotional intensity, intimacy, or even inappropriate remarks simply because fatigue has diminished our mental guardrails.

Why Boundaries Matter

If a structured and clear conversation does not start off as intended, it is almost inevitable that as the hours wear on, boundaries will blur. Prolonged exposure to emotional dialogue in a relaxed, late-night setting creates the perfect environment for impulsive behavior. The longer the conversation extends beyond a reasonable cutoff time—traditionally set at 11 p.m.—the greater the risk that intentions become muddled and actions might stray from the true purpose of Courtship.

Beyond the immediate impact on conversation quality, late-night exchanges reveal deeper aspects of a person's lifestyle. Consider this: if someone frequently insists on staying up late to talk, what does that indicate about their overall time management, discipline, and daily structure? Are they productive individuals with well-defined goals, or do they operate on a schedule driven by impulse and emotional gratification? A disciplined schedule is a sign of maturity and responsibility—qualities essential for building a stable, long-term relationship.

The Benefits of a Clear Cutoff

Agreeing to end all communication by 11 p.m. is more than just a rule—it's a sign of respect and discipline. It demonstrates that both parties are serious about the process and are not simply engaging in casual, emotionally charged exchanges that can lead to confusion or premature attachment. This boundary prevents the conversation from being hijacked by fatigue-driven emotions, ensuring that interactions remain intentional, measured, and aligned with the core values of Courtship.

Moreover, establishing this cutoff has practical benefits. It creates a natural pause that forces both individuals to step back and reflect on the conversation. With a clear end time, there is time to process thoughts, avoid impulsive reactions, and approach the next day's interactions with a refreshed, rational perspective. This pause helps keep the relationship grounded and prevents emotional overload, allowing both individuals to cherish and build on the connection at a sustainable pace.

A Reflection on Personal Responsibility

Late-night conversations often become a mirror reflecting a person's habits and lifestyle. If someone consistently disregards a reasonable cutoff, it may signal a lack of discipline or an inability to manage their time responsibly. Such behavior might indicate that they are not fully committed to the principles of Courtship, which are designed to build a strong foundation for a lasting relationship.

Respecting this boundary is a clear indication that an individual values structure and maturity—not just in their interactions with you but in their overall approach to life.

For those who persist in late-night exchanges despite knowing the guidelines, it is a red flag. It suggests a disregard for the agreed-upon structure and possibly a deeper unwillingness to prioritize long-term commitment over momentary emotional highs. In the context of Courtship, where the focus is on building genuine understanding and mutual respect, such behavior can be detrimental.

Embracing the Process

Part of the journey of truly getting to know someone is understanding that meaningful connections cannot—and should not—be rushed. Building a deep, lasting relationship takes time, patience, and discipline. By shutting down communication at a set time, both parties are compelled to slow down and savor the process of getting to know each other without the pressure of constant, late-night exchanges.

I have been married for sixteen years, and even now, I continue to learn new things about my wife as she learns about me. This ongoing discovery underscores that understanding develops gradually through patient, disciplined effort. There is great wisdom in these guidelines. If you strive to avoid knee-jerk emotional reactions, you will witness that wisdom unfold in your own life. Trust the process, remain disciplined, and allow time to work its magic. Be patient, and true understanding will eventually come.

CHAPTER FOUR

THE WHO? OF COURTSHIP

Key Definitions:

Who: What or which person or people?

Preference: A greater liking for one alternative over another or others.

Catfish: To lure someone into a relationship by means of a fictional online persona.

Spectrum: A way to classify something in terms of its position on a scale between two extremes or opposites.

Balance: An even distribution that enables someone or something to remain upright and steady; a state where different elements are equal or in proper proportion.

When it comes to love, the "who" you choose to court is a matter of personal preference. No one can dictate whom you should be attracted to or determine what type of person should catch your eye. Naturally, our initial attention is drawn to physical appearance. There is no denying that attraction plays a significant role in sparking interest—how someone presents themselves visually often reflects, to some degree, how they view themselves. The way a person carries themselves, their grooming, style, and even their posture can communicate confidence, self-respect, or, conversely, a lack thereof. While physical attraction is a necessary starting point, it must not be the sole foundation upon which a relationship is built.

Looks can be deceiving. In today's world, many are highly skilled at curating an image—through social media, filters, cosmetic enhancements, and carefully crafted online personas—to appeal to specific audiences. This image, designed for personal validation, financial gain, or even deception, may not align with who they truly are. Thus, it becomes critical to look beyond what the eyes can see and to focus on the substance beneath the surface.

Consider shows like Catfish or the Netflix documentary The Tinder Swindler. These narratives powerfully illustrate how individuals can become so captivated by an illusion that they willingly ignore red flags, dismiss common sense, and override their instincts. When physical attraction and emotional manipulation dominate, our capacity for logic diminishes, leading us down paths that often end in deception, heartbreak, and even financial or emotional ruin.

This is where the true value of the courtship process becomes evident. Courtship is not just about dating; it is about truly seeing the person before you. It provides the opportunity to witness the full spectrum of an individual—their ups and downs, strengths and weaknesses, habits and inconsistencies. Through Courtship, you can observe how extreme a person is in their self-perception. Ask yourself: Are they overly obsessed with their looks? Do they derive their entire sense of worth from external appearance? Are they so self-absorbed that it clouds their ability to form a genuine, balanced relationship? These critical observations help determine whether someone is a suitable long-term partner or if their traits become deal breakers. Perhaps you share similar qualities, and the connection proves harmonious, or maybe the differences prompt essential conversations. Either way, the courtship process ensures you are not merely relying on superficial attraction but are engaging in a comprehensive assessment of true compatibility.

This book is an introduction—a guide designed to sharpen your discernment so that you can see with your "third eye" rather than relying solely on your physical senses. It equips you with the tools to see beyond illusions and to make informed, rational decisions about whom to invite into your life. The real questions you should be asking go far deeper than appearances: How does this person act under pressure? How do they respond to adversity? How do they handle significant decisions? What motivates them? In essence, how do they think? These factors are what ultimately determine long-term compatibility. Physical attraction will always be a factor, but it should never be the only criterion. Courtship offers clarity, patience, and perspective so that your decision for a lifelong commitment is made with both heart and mind fully engaged.

Another poignant example comes from the lyrics of Lauryn Hill, who once said, "What you want may make you cry, and what you need may pass you by." These words reveal the emotional struggle between desire and necessity. In relationships, it is easy to be drawn to what we want—the charming personality, the attractive face, the smooth words, or even the status someone carries. Yet, these qualities do not always translate into what we truly need for long-term success. Courtship is designed to help you balance desire with need, ensuring that temporary emotions do not overshadow what is essential for a fulfilling partnership.

The community to which the "who" belongs is also of paramount importance. A true community provides structure—a way of life that the person you are considering is naturally part of. The strength of a community lies in its ability to give you a broader understanding of an individual beyond their personal presentation. When someone is an active, committed member of a community, that community offers valuable insights into their reputation, behavior, and interactions with others. Even if you are not blood relatives, a genuine community acts like an extended family. It provides perspectives from aunts, uncles, grandparents, siblings, and other married couples who have observed the person in various settings over time.

Many spiritual texts speak about being "evenly yoked." In today's context, this phrase extends beyond mere spiritual alignment. In our modern era, we cannot rely solely on spiritual compatibility when choosing a partner. We must ask ourselves tough questions: How committed am I to my own community? Is the person I am courting similarly dedicated? Do we share the same values, principles, and life vision? These questions are crucial because the community one belongs to significantly shapes worldview, habits, and priorities. Although acknowledging the Originator in all things is a powerful foundation, community need not be strictly spirituality-based. It might form around shared lifestyles or values—such as veganism, a passion for biking, the discipline of armed services, or the cooperative nature of homeschooling. When like-minded individuals unite around a common way of life, they form a community that provides both structure and accountability.

Of course, many genuinely good people exist outside of any formal community, and that is perfectly acceptable. While being community-oriented is not the only path to finding a quality partner, it does offer additional layers of support and insight. In today's casual relationship landscape, where long-term vision is often lacking, the structured approach of Courtship can be invaluable. Whether you meet someone at a grocery store, in a library, at a park, or during a family gathering, I hope that you use the powerful tool of Courtship. It is more than just a process—it is a form of protection, clarity, and intentionality.

Courtship empowers you to see beyond fleeting physical attraction and to focus on what truly matters in a lifelong partnership. It enables you to balance emotions and desires with logic, wisdom, and true compatibility. Ultimately, when you choose a partner through Courtship, you do so with purpose, awareness, and confidence, making a well-informed decision that aligns with your highest good.

CHAPTER FIVE

THE WHEN? OF COURTSHIP

Key Definitions:

When: At what time? The moment or period during which something occurs.

Time: (Verb) To plan, schedule, or arrange when something should happen.

(Noun) The indefinite, continuous progression of existence and events that occur in the past, present, and future as a whole.

Attract: To cause someone to come to a place or participate in a venture by offering something of interest, favorable conditions, or opportunities.

Heal: To make free from injury or disease; to restore to soundness or wholeness, returning something to its original purity or integrity.

Question: A prompt to examine: When was your most

recent relationship? Are there any lingering feelings or ongoing communication with an ex?

Time is one of the most important factors in healing. Before entering into courtship, it is essential to be free from the emotional and mental attachments of past relationships—for at least a year, ideally. This period allows both individuals the space to reflect on their experiences, to process and learn from them, and ultimately to heal. Investing your emotions, energy, and future into someone who remains entangled with a past relationship creates uncertainty, insecurity, and instability. Such unresolved issues are destructive forces in a relationship intended to last a lifetime. If you still harbor lingering feelings or unresolved emotions or maintain open lines of communication with an ex, it is critical that you do not move forward. Starting something new under those conditions only sets the stage for recurring pain, accumulating baggage, and an endless cycle of unresolved issues. It is not fair to you, nor is it fair to the person with whom you may eventually enter into courtship.

Healing from past relationship drama is crucial for truly knowing yourself. The past shapes us in profound ways that we sometimes fail to recognize until we take the time to sit with it, process it, and ultimately heal. Life's trials—whether stemming from family secrets, generational patterns, abuse, the absence of supportive figures, or painful past relationships—leave wounds that do not simply vanish. These experiences become embedded deep within our consciousness, influencing our behaviors, triggers, and even our expectations in relationships. Identifying, confronting, and addressing these wounds is essential; healing cannot be rushed. It requires dedicated time, self-reflection, and often a great deal of patience and forgiveness. Without this process, we risk carrying these unaddressed issues into marriage, where they may manifest in unforeseen and damaging ways.

Courtship itself provides natural stages during which these difficult discussions can occur. It is not only about discovering the appealing, fun, or exciting facets of a person; it is also about understanding their journey—their struggles, the scars they bear, and how they have worked (or are still working) to overcome their past. Equally important is that both parties feel safe and comfortable enough to open up about these sensitive issues. The goal is not to unload pain onto one another but to create a space where honesty, transparency, and mutual understanding can take root. Timing is crucial; introducing these topics too early might lead to resistance, yet avoiding them altogether will eventually result in greater misunderstandings and unresolved conflict.

I understand that these topics are incredibly difficult to bring up, let alone share with a potential life partner. Many of these experiences are deeply personal, and exposing your vulnerabilities to someone you are just beginning to know can feel overwhelming. However, if progress is being made, these conversations must eventually occur. There is no way around addressing them if the goal is to forge a healthy, lasting, and authentic marriage. Both parties should agree that it is far preferable to understand each other's pasts early on rather than face the consequences three, five, or even ten years into a marriage. Today, far too many invest years in a union only to later unearth deep-rooted issues that were never addressed, resulting in resentment, pain, and emotional distance. When such issues emerge, the opportunity to heal has often been lost. If both individuals are committed, then it is imperative to heal and overcome past pains before proceeding. Wouldn't it be better to have taken the necessary time prior to marriage, ensuring that both parties are truly ready and fully aware of each other's realities?

Time is not merely something to be passed; it is a resource—a precious gift that plays a vital role in healing and preparation. Without taking the time to reflect, to work on oneself, and to engage in meaningful, structured conversations during courtship, you risk building a marriage on unstable ground. This process ensures that both individuals step into their future together with clarity, readiness, and a commitment based not only on fleeting emotions but on a solid foundation of understanding, trust, and a shared vision for a strong, enduring partnership.

Rethinking the Timeline for Marriage

When it comes to marriage, you often hear all kinds of advice—much of it laden with hesitation, doubt, and even outright discouragement. "You're too young; live your life, travel the world; don't do it—are you sure?" These are common refrains when the topic of marriage arises, especially for those who express an interest in committing at a younger age. But if we're being honest with ourselves, what are our true options? Do we choose to remain celibate, focus on personal growth, and work diligently on becoming the best version of ourselves with the goal of marriage in mind? Or do we flirt with fleeting romances, engage in aimless dating, and prolong a cycle of short-term relationships and temporary pleasures until our thirties?

Time waits for no one. Society often conditions us to believe that our twenties are meant for wild adventures, endless experiences, and a steadfast avoidance of serious commitments. Yet, when we pause and truly reflect, we must ask whether that mindset actually benefits us in the long run. How many individuals in their late twenties or thirties find themselves emotionally exhausted, burdened with baggage from past relationships, or struggling to find a partner who is genuinely ready to build something lasting? The illusion of unlimited time can lead to wasted years in situations that were never meant to endure. If the goal is a strong, fulfilling marriage, why delay the process of preparation? Why not begin with intentionality early on rather than waiting until later in life to try to shift habits, heal wounds, and unlearn detrimental behaviors?

When we encounter someone, who is vehemently against marriage, it is essential not to take their words at face value. Instead, we should ask deeper questions: What led them to that mindset? How did their own marriage—or the marriages they observed—begin? Did they become physically involved too soon? Were critical warning signs ignored?

More often than not, a closer look reveals that marriage itself wasn't the problem. Rather, the issues lay in the choices made before marriage—the foundation that was weak or never truly established. Many with negative perceptions of marriage simply never received the tools, guidance, or discipline necessary to enter into it properly. They rushed in fueled by infatuation, overlooked red flags, and allowed emotions and physical desires to cloud their judgment. Instead of acknowledging where things went wrong, they end up placing the blame on the concept of marriage itself.

The proper path is to cultivate a deep love for yourself while continually committing to self-improvement. Better yourself, build your character, strengthen your mind, and refine your values. When genuine attraction arises, be prepared to handle it with wisdom rather than pure impulse. If attraction occurs, do not let emotions lead you blindly—instead, rely on the tools of courtship. Let structure and discipline guide your decisions rather than fleeting feelings or superficial desires.

It is essential to introduce these tools from the very beginning. Establishing clear boundaries and expectations upfront forms the very foundation upon which a meaningful relationship can be built. Courtship should not be an afterthought or a late-stage addition to a relationship—it must be laid out as the groundwork from the start. If someone is genuinely interested in a serious, meaningful partnership, they will not be intimidated by structure; rather, they will respect and embrace it.

The very first test in any courtship is observing how well the other person responds to the process. Do they recognize its value? Do they respect the discipline and intentionality that come with it? Most importantly, do they understand that courtship is designed to protect both individuals by ensuring that the relationship is built on a solid foundation rather than on transient emotional highs and physical gratification? The initial sign is their willingness to move forward, showing openness to doing things differently and choosing a path that demands patience, self-control, and maturity. If they dismiss, discredit, or blow off these principles as unnecessary, that response alone provides a clear indicator of where they stand and what they prioritize. In such cases, it is essential to stand by your own principles and keep moving forward. There is no need to convince, explain, or justify the process to someone unwilling to receive it. The discipline of courtship is not for everyone—it is for those who are truly ready to build something meaningful and lasting.

At the end of the day, marriage is not something to be feared, delayed, or avoided. It is a sacred union that, when entered into with wisdom and preparation, has the power to bring immense joy, stability, and fulfillment. The key is not just to find someone who wants to be married but to find someone who is willing to do the necessary work to prepare for marriage. Time should never be wasted on individuals who are not ready, not serious, or not aligned with the same vision. Recognizing this early on allows you to redirect your energy toward what is truly meant for you.

When should you enter into a courtship? This is a valid question that demands deep thought and self-reflection. The word "when" is closely tied to the concept of time—one of the most crucial elements in this process. "When" happens when both parties are genuinely tired of the games and have reached a point of clarity and recognize that their current approach isn't yielding the results they truly desire. The appropriate "when" is marked by a disinterest in shallow connections and meaningless interactions—a time when both individuals understand that their past choices, repeated cycles, and endured heartaches were lessons meant to guide them toward a higher level of awareness. The realization is that love and commitment require more than fleeting feelings; they demand preparation, responsibility, and intentionality.

I recall a conversation with a brother who said something that forever changed my perspective: "Bro. Kobie, Allah has someone for you, but He is not going to bring her into your life under your current conditions." That statement resonated deeply and applies to both men and women. Too often, we become so consumed with searching and scanning for the right person that we forget it's not about looking—it's about being. When you chase after someone, you often do so from a place of lack. However, when you truly value and know yourself, you naturally shine. A confident, purpose-driven individual doesn't have to chase; instead, the right person is drawn to that light. Focus on who you are becoming: work on your mindset, discipline, emotional stability, and spiritual connection. When these aspects align, attraction happens naturally.

But attraction alone is not enough; it must be followed by structure, principles, and standards. As a man, I firmly believe there are fundamental standards that should be in place even before entering into a courtship. When should a man begin courting? When his walk with God is evident in his actions, decisions, and demeanor. When he recognizes that God is all-knowing and all-seeing and that no decision should be made without seeking divine guidance when he has established reliable transportation, a stable living situation, and a consistent source of income, that reflects his drive for financial security. When he understands the weight of responsibility that comes with leading a household—not only financially, but mentally, physically, and spiritually. What kind of drive does he have to earn his own money and build something that makes him independent and self-sufficient? Does he grasp how critical security is for a woman—not just financially, but in every aspect of life? This is fundamental, not negotiable. One meaning of the word "husband" is to take care of something that does not belong to him. A wife does not belong to a man; she belongs to God. Yet, it is the husband's responsibility to protect, provide for, and nurture the woman entrusted to him by God. That is a weighty assignment, one that comes with deep accountability. If she wishes to contribute in her unique way, that is acceptable, but the responsibility of securing and leading the household falls on the man. He must be ready to carry that weight—not to complain or hesitate, but to embrace it fully.

On the flip side, when is the "when" for the woman? What qualifies her to enter into a courtship? Is it simply measured by tangible markers such as having her own place or a stable source of income? The truth is, while a man may build a house, a woman creates a home. A home is shaped by her vision, spirit, and nurturing ability. Her essence transforms four walls into a sanctuary of peace, comfort, and love. Just as we evaluate a man's walk with God through his actions, decisions, and level of responsibility, we must also consider a woman's spiritual journey. Can you see it in her temperament, the way she speaks, how she carries herself and interacts with others? A good wife is not only a partner but also a reflection of the man's own commitment and vision. The type of woman a man attracts is often a direct mirror of his energy, mindset, and readiness to take on responsibility.

For a husband, it is crucial to always consider the future—what is to come, what needs care, and how to ensure that his family is secure. Equally important is asking, "What kind of mother will my wife be?" Will she have the time and emotional capacity to nurture our children, guide them, and be actively present in their development? Will she be their first teacher, laying the foundation for values and character before the wider world exerts its influence? As a husband, ensuring that I can provide not only materially but also create an environment where my wife is free to focus on motherhood is paramount. These are not outdated questions;

they are vital considerations that shape the structure of a family and the legacy that emerges through marriage. A good husband cherishes a home filled with peace, comfort, and holistic nourishment—qualities that stem from a wife who is aligned with the household's vision.

I also want to take a moment to reflect on timing in relation to our children and pre-adults. As parents, we naturally look back on our own relationships, our choices, and the lessons learned—often through trial and error. Many of us carry regrets about relationships, certain decisions, or the time we wasted on people and situations that were never meant for us. We do not want our children to repeat these same mistakes. We do not wish for them to experience unnecessary trials, heartbreaks, or losses.

In a society where many are told to "wait" and "live their lives first," we must question what that truly means. What exactly are young people supposed to be waiting for? When is the right time? If a young man and woman are spiritually, emotionally, and mentally prepared—if they possess the necessary tools, mindset, and structure to build something meaningful—why should they spend 5, 10, or even 15 years trapped in dead-end relationships that only accumulate baggage they will later have to heal from? The prevailing narrative pushes the idea that love should be delayed and commitment feared, but what if we introduced our youth to a different model?

What if we showed them courtship as a viable pathway—one where they can start young, work together, build together, and overcome trials as a united team rather than entering marriage burdened by past mistakes? Let's get this knowledge into the hands of our youth and pre-adults so they see that there is a better way than the fleeting relationships the world often promotes. Let's teach them that love when built on a strong foundation of discipline, intentionality, and mutual growth, is not something to fear, delay, or avoid. When the time is right, they won't have to search endlessly; they simply need to be ready.

CHAPTER SIX

THE HOW? OF COURTSHIP

Key Definitions:

How: In what way or manner; by what means? For example, "How does this work?" or "How do I fix this?"

Respect: A deep admiration for someone or something, typically elicited by their abilities, qualities, or achievements.

Elders: Leaders or senior figures—male or female—in a family, tribe, or community.

How Do I Start a Courtship?

If someone shows interest, the first step is to determine whether they are equally interested in a structured, intentional courtship rather than casual dating. Honesty and direct communication are essential from the very beginning. Express your attraction, but also make it clear that your approach to relationships is different—you are interested in courtship, which comes with intention, structure, and purpose. It is not about short-term fun; it is about establishing long-term compatibility and commitment. When you initiate contact, be upfront: let them know you find them attractive and ask if they would be willing to engage in a courtship process rather than traditional dating. This early clarity sets the tone for everything that follows.

Honoring Tradition: Involving Family and Community

Historically—and still in some cultures today—it was considered a sign of respect and protection for a man to approach a woman only after first consulting a trusted male figure in her family. This tradition was never about control or outdated customs; it was about honor, respect, and safeguarding the woman. In times past, men recognized that a woman's family played a vital role in screening and guiding the courtship process, ensuring that she was approached with sincere intentions.

I often tell my daughters that whenever they have questions about boys, they should come to me because I understand how boys think—I was one once myself. Just as women naturally understand other women, men have an inherent ability to understand their own kind. A young woman may not always recognize certain tactics, behaviors, or warning signs that a more experienced male figure in her life would catch. That is why involving a woman's father figure—or another respected male role model such as her grandfather, uncle, older brother, or pastor—is essential. This step is not a declaration of marriage or an immediate commitment; rather, it is laying the groundwork for respect and acknowledging the family and community that have shaped her.

For a man expressing genuine interest, stepping forward and asking to meet these important figures sends a powerful message: "I am ready to take on the role of protector, provider, and leader." This is a significant responsibility that should not be taken lightly. For fathers and male guardians, this moment is not about ego but about recognition and responsibility. A man who is serious about courting must be willing to honor this process and meet the people who have been instrumental in shaping the woman he wishes to court. Conversely, a man who resists or avoids this process might be signaling ill intentions. If he refuses to go through proper channels, a woman should ask herself: Why does he want me but not want to meet those who raised me? What is he trying to avoid, and what might his motives be? A man who genuinely values and respects a woman will naturally respect the people who love and care for her.

Observing Character and Values

The "How" of starting a courtship begins with careful observation. Before anything else, observe the person's character, habits, mindset, and values. Courtship is not about rushing into a relationship; it is about taking intentional, measured steps. If a man is serious about a woman, he will invest time in observing her actions, temperament, and how she interacts with the world. Likewise, a woman should assess a man's character, consistency, work ethic, and overall demeanor. Sometimes, men notice qualities in other men that women might overlook, and vice versa. This is why the input from trusted community members and mentors is invaluable.

At some point during the courtship, it is natural and necessary to introduce the person you are interested into someone you hold dear—a mentor, an elder, or a father figure. For instance, if a man values the counsel of a respected mentor or a family patriarch, introducing the woman he is courting to that individual can provide both a blessing and additional perspective. The same holds true for women. Having the blessing and insight of those with life experience can serve as a crucial litmus test in determining long-term compatibility.

The Importance of Structure and Guidance

Courtship is a process built on structure and discipline. It requires both parties to engage in thoughtful communication guided by established boundaries and mutual respect. This structured approach is what differentiates courtship from casual dating; it is designed to safeguard both individuals, ensuring that the relationship develops on a solid foundation. By setting clear expectations and introducing trusted mentors and family members early on, both partners have the opportunity to be seen fully and honestly. In doing so, they can assess not only immediate attraction but also long-term potential for a lasting, meaningful union.

This is all part of the process—but it must be done with logic, patience, and common sense. We don't meet someone today and then, a week later, declare, "Hey, we're courting, so you need to meet my entire family and my spiritual mentor." That is not how courtship works. Instead, we must feel the natural flow of the process and respect its distinct stages of development. Every relationship unfolds at its own pace, and wisdom lies in knowing when to introduce someone into deeper circles of trust. Timing is everything. The goal is to build with clarity, not to rush blindly into something before the foundation has been properly laid.

In the end, the "how" of starting a courtship is about intentionality, respect, and order. It is about setting a standard from the very beginning and ensuring that both parties are aligned in their values and intentions. It means honoring the process rather than skipping essential steps. The foundation of a strong marriage begins with the principles and structure of a proper courtship. When done correctly, this process not only protects both individuals from unnecessary heartbreak but also leads them toward a purposeful, lasting, and fulfilling union.

Before moving to the next question of "Why," let's take a moment to pivot into nature. Look at courtship in the animal kingdom: the Adélie penguin collects the finest stones, the peacock jumping spider performs its elaborate dance, and the Satin Bowerbird constructs an intricately decorated bower. In these examples, nature has established a rhythm where the male takes the initiative to display his worthiness, setting the stage for the partnership.

This same principle applies in real life. A man should have his own standards—steady, reliable income (whether self-made or through a stable 9-to-5), secure living arrangements that point toward homeownership, and reliable transportation. Stability is not just about financial security; it's about demonstrating responsibility, discipline, and a commitment to personal growth. These foundational elements are not merely for attracting a woman; they signify readiness for the responsibilities that come with leading, protecting, and providing for a family.

At this point, some may ask, "What am I doing all of this for? What does she have to do?" It's a fair question—one that has been asked time and again. Consider the weight of preparation, effort, and struggle. Before answering, reflect: Have you ever heard an elder or a trusted friend say, "Man, she was a good woman," with a tone heavy with regret? I recall a close friend recounting a past relationship, nearly in tears with remorse for having let something rare slip away. It wasn't about material things or status; it was about something deeper and irreplaceable.

A good woman is more than just a partner—she is an amplifier of a man's potential. She has the ability to nurture, heal, and elevate you, even in your darkest moments. She is the one who can transform a house into a home—a sanctuary of love, wisdom, and peace. A good woman becomes the first teacher of your children, shaping the next generation with values, love, and unwavering support. She provides balance—a strong, graceful, and encouraging presence that reminds you of what truly matters, helping you maintain your vision while grounding you in reality.

So, keep these jewels in mind as you continue on your journey. Understand that courtship, preparation, and the effort you invest are not merely about winning someone's attention; they are about being truly ready to walk alongside a good woman—one who will multiply your strengths, sharpen your mind, and bring peace to your soul. Just as nature follows its intricate, purposeful design for courtship and partnership, life, too, moves in a similar rhythm. Every step of preparation is never in vain, and the reward of building a strong, lasting union with the right partner is well worth the journey.

CHAPTER SEVEN

COURTSHIP IN NATURE

Scriptural Reflections:

Holy Bible: Job 12:7-10

7. "But ask now the beasts, and they shall teach thee, and the fowls of the air, and they shall tell thee:"

8. "Or speak to the earth, and it shall teach thee: and the fishes of the sea shall declare unto thee."

9. "Who knoweth not in all these that the hand of the Lord hath wrought this?"

10. "In whose hand is the soul of every living thing, and the breath of mankind."

Holy Quran: Chapter 45, Verses 3-4

3. "The fact is that there are signs for believers in the heavens and in the earth,"

4. "And for the people who have firm faith, there are signs

in your own creation and (in) that of all (living) creatures which He spreads abroad."

These sacred texts remind us that the natural world is a profound teacher. Its patterns, including those of courtship, reveal the underlying order and wisdom of creation.

Courtship in the Animal Kingdom

Courtship behavior is vital in an animal's life as it allows both sexes to choose a partner and engage in a behavioral ritual that ultimately results in successful copulation. Courtship displays are specific behavioral patterns that reoccur during the mating period, with various individuals of the same species exhibiting comparable behaviors. This process is fundamental in ensuring the continuation of a species, as it not only facilitates reproduction but also plays a significant role in natural selection. By choosing mates based on particular characteristics, animals contribute to the overall fitness of their offspring, ensuring that advantageous traits are passed down to future generations.

The Role of Female Choice

Females devote far more time and energy to reproduction than males. This disparity stems from the biological investment required for processes such as gestation, egg-laying, and parental care. As a result, females are more inclined to be choosy about partners. The selection of a mate is not arbitrary; rather, it is guided by traits that indicate strength, genetic superiority, or the ability to provide essential resources. In many species, females prefer males who are bigger or exhibit more pronounced masculine characteristics than their rivals. These traits often serve as indicators of good health, robust genetics, and the capacity to dominate in competitive scenarios.

Male Competition and Display

Sometimes, males participate in physical fighting, engaging in direct combat with rivals to establish dominance and secure mating rights. These battles can be intense—often resulting in injuries or even death—but they serve a critical function in determining the strongest and most capable individuals within a population. In addition to physical confrontations, males employ other strategies such as displaying vibrant physical colors, performing acrobatics, and engaging in elaborate dances. These displays serve as a testament to their fitness, endurance, and ability to perform under pressure. Some males even resort to alternative tactics like vocalizations, nest-building, or offering food as gifts to attract a mate. Although these behaviors vary widely, they all serve the fundamental purpose of increasing the chances of being chosen by a female.

The Evolutionary Dance

In general, the more striking and impressive the male displays, the more likely he is to be chosen as a mate. Whether through physical prowess, vibrant coloration, or intricate rituals, males must stand out to capture the attention of potential mates. This dynamic interplay between male competition and female choice drives the evolution of exaggerated traits and behaviors, ensuring that those who succeed in courtship pass on their genes to future generations.

I could write volumes about the courtships in the animal kingdom—exploring the fascinating ways in which species have evolved unique strategies for attracting mates. However, for the sake of time, I'm going to pull up three examples to look into. These cases will provide a deeper understanding of the diversity and complexity of courtship behaviors, illustrating how different species navigate the intricate dance of reproduction and selection.

The Adélie Penguin

Antarctica's coastline and nearby islands are breeding grounds for Adélie penguins. These resilient birds thrive in one of the harshest environments on Earth, enduring extreme cold and formidable winds as they return year after year to continue their species' cycle of life. The Adélie penguins return to the Antarctic's rocky terrain between October and early November, a period that marks the beginning of their intricate and fascinating courtship rituals. The males arrive first, staking their claim on nesting sites and beginning the meticulous process of constructing their nests before the females follow. This initial behavior is crucial, as the availability of a well-built nest can significantly influence a female's choice of mate.

The nicest rocks and pebbles that a penguin can find are used to construct its nest, a process that requires patience, determination, and, at times, even aggression. When they find the ideal stone, they will roll it back to their nest or, if it is tiny enough, carry it in their beak. These carefully chosen stones serve as the very building blocks of their nesting sites, arranged to create a secure environment for their future offspring. The competition for these precious pebbles is intense, as the smoothest and most well-formed stones not only provide structural benefits but also hold symbolic importance in the courtship process. In fact, they may even steal stones from neighbors and engage in fierce skirmishes, underscoring just how valuable these pebbles are in the eyes of potential mates. This competitive and sometimes ruthless behavior highlights the stones' dual role in both practicality and mating success.The male gives the female a pebble as a gift during courtship—an offering that serves as both a practical contribution to nest-building and a gesture of affection. This exchange is more than a simple transaction; it is laden with meaning. Acceptance of the pebble signifies trust, compatibility, and commitment between the two penguins, reinforcing the bond that will help them navigate the challenges of parenthood together in the extreme Antarctic conditions.

Male Adélie penguins also perform a ritualized display known as the "salute," which is an essential part of their courtship strategy. During this display, a male positions himself about four meters away from the female he is interested in, ensuring that she has a clear view of his presence and intentions. He then exhibits his maximum height, stretching his body to its full length to appear as imposing and impressive as possible. His posture, enhanced by beak thrusting and an arched neck, serves not only to attract the female's attention but also to assert dominance over his territory. In doing so, he signals that he is prepared to defend his nesting site and his chosen mate.

The courtship process of Adélie penguins is a remarkable blend of strategic competition, symbolic gestures, and steadfast commitment. These birds engage in acts of perseverance, devotion, and even rivalry to secure both a mate and a stable nest, ensuring the best possible conditions for raising their young. Through stone gifting, salutes, and fierce determination, Adélie penguins exemplify the depth and complexity of courtship behaviors in the animal kingdom, demonstrating that even in the icy wilderness of Antarctica, love and partnership play a crucial role in survival.

The Peacock Jumping Spider

The male peacock jumping spider, despite being about the size of a grain of rice, is a master of dazzling courtship displays and is found in Australia. This tiny yet vibrant arachnid relies on his striking appearance and meticulously choreographed dance moves to win over a potential mate. Male spiders typically display the brilliantly colored upper surface of their abdomen—often adorned with extensions and fringes—in elaborate courtship dances. These vibrant colors and intricate movements serve both as a visual spectacle and as a means of communication, signaling his fitness and desirability.

The colors on these spiders are produced by two main methods. One involves pigments that generate reds, whites, and creams on barbed scales to scatter light and create contrast, while the production of blues relies on arrays of nanostructures embedded in flat, convex, sac-like scales. These nanostructures reflect light at specific wavelengths, producing a shiny, sometimes violet-blue hue that intensifies their iridescence. This complex biological mechanism gives the male peacock jumping spider his mesmerizing appearance, making him an unforgettable sight during his courtship ritual.

The male must dance for his life—quite literally. His survival and reproductive success hinge on his ability to impress a highly selective female. To woo her and avoid being eaten, he performs an intricate dance, displaying a brilliantly colored fan attached to his abdomen while rhythmically waving his legs. Every step, movement, and posture is carefully timed to convey his health, agility, and genetic superiority. This courtship performance can last up to 50 minutes, an extended display that ultimately determines whether he passes on his genes or becomes a meal for the discerning female. The stakes are high, and every male must put forth his best performance to increase his chances of survival.

The peacock jumping spider's courtship process is not only a fascinating example of natural selection but also a metaphor for life itself—where skill, effort, and the ability to stand out can determine one's fate. In this tiny yet extraordinary creature, the beauty and brutality of nature coexist, reminding us that success often comes down to one's ability to impress, adapt, and perform under pressure

Blue Satin Bowerbird

The Satin Bowerbird is considered one of the most intelligent birds in nature, displaying remarkable problem-solving skills, memory, and creativity. These birds are known not only for their striking appearance but also for their extraordinary courtship behaviors, which involve a complex and artistic process designed solely to attract a mate. When not foraging, the male bowerbird dedicates himself to building intricate mating grounds called "bowers"—an endeavor that demands both patience and architectural skill. Unlike traditional nests, bowers are decorative structures used only for courtship, meant to impress potential mates rather than to raise young.

The construction of these bowers is an art form. Males meticulously arrange and fine-tune their creations with twigs, berries, flowers, and feathers to ensure they stand out. Once the basic structure is complete, the male decorates his bower with saliva, charcoal, and any attractive object he can find. In areas near human habitats, Satin Bowerbirds are known to incorporate man-made items—particularly those of a blue hue—such as plastic caps, straws, and pieces of fabric. This fascination with blue is so intense that males will even steal prized decorations from one another to outshine their rivals.

Once satisfied with his bower, the male turns his attention to the next phase of courtship. When females are nearby, he prances and struts around his carefully crafted avenue, moving with exaggerated, almost theatrical precision. Every movement is deliberate, designed to highlight his agility, confidence, and overall fitness. As part of his performance, he presents the female with various gifts—leaves, berries, and the prized blue trinkets he has painstakingly gathered. These offerings extend the aesthetic of his bower and serve as tokens of his dedication and resourcefulness. Accompanying these gestures are a series of unusual vocalizations—hissing and chattering noises that add to the theatricality of his display.

If the female is pleased with both the male and his bower, she will indicate her acceptance by choosing to mate with him within the bower itself. This act signifies that his display was compelling enough to win her over. Once mating is complete, however, the female takes sole responsibility for nesting and raising the young, leaving the male to continue maintaining and improving his bower for future courtship opportunities. In the world of the Satin Bowerbird, the male's role is that of a performer and architect, ensuring that his genetic legacy endures by outshining his competition.

The courtship process of the Satin Bowerbird is a fascinating demonstration of intelligence, creativity, and persistence. These birds have evolved to use artistic expression and problem-solving, as much as physical strength or vocal prowess, to succeed in mating. Their ability to manipulate their environment, adapt to human presence, and engage in highly specialized behaviors showcases the complexity and diversity of natural courtship strategies. The lengths to which a male will go—constructing, decorating, dancing, and even stealing—to impress a female highlight the importance of aesthetic appeal and performance in the natural world. Through this remarkable display, the Satin Bowerbird stands as a testament to the intricate and sometimes theatrical nature of animal courtship, proving that love, in its many forms, is as much about creativity as it is about survival.

In Closing…

Let these examples from nature remind us that the principles of courtship are universal. Whether it's a tiny jumping spider or a creatively ingenious bowerbird, the drive to attract a mate through displays of strength, beauty, and resourcefulness underscores the importance of preparation and performance. Just as these animals follow natural, structured processes to secure their futures, so too must we approach our relationships with intentionality and discipline. The lessons of nature—its blend of beauty and brutality—offer timeless wisdom: true success in love and life is achieved when we combine skill, effort, and the courage to stand out. Embrace these insights as you continue your journey, knowing that every thoughtful, deliberate step brings you closer to a lasting, meaningful partnership.

CHAPTER EIGHT

THE WHY? IN COURTSHIP

Of all the questions to ask, "Why?" is the one wrapped in wisdom and understanding. It is a question that invites us to reflect on purpose and value—not only in our relationships but also in the legacy we wish to pass on. Why should I, or even my pre-adult teenager, consider courting rather than dating? As stated in previous chapters, courtship is for mature audiences only. It is for those who are tired of the games, headaches, and losses that often come with casual dating.

Why Court?

Because courtship demonstrates self-value, when you choose to court instead of date, you make a conscious decision to approach relationships with intentionality and purpose rather than being swept away by fleeting emotions or momentary attractions. Courtship is built on self-respect, discipline, and a clear understanding of one's worth. It ensures that both individuals are not merely testing the waters but are seeking a connection rooted in deeper compatibility, shared values, and a vision for the future. By prioritizing commitment and mutual respect, you lay the foundation for a relationship based not solely on transient feelings but on a well-thought-out decision to pursue a meaningful and lasting partnership.

Instilling Values for Future Generations

By modeling and instilling these principles in our own lives, we help our children understand that love is not just about passion or momentary emotions; it's about dedication, understanding, and a willingness to grow together. Our children learn that relationships should be driven by discernment, patience, and wisdom—not by impulse. When we teach them to value themselves, they are more likely to enter relationships with confidence, security, and a strong sense of self-worth rather than seeking validation through casual, superficial connections.

Reflecting Our Priorities

What we value in life often aligns with what we love. Our priorities, goals, and the way we invest our time and energy reflect the things that hold significance in our lives. If stability, trust, and respect are among our highest values, our approach to relationships must mirror these principles. Courtship aligns with this perspective by prioritizing emotional and spiritual connections over temporary gratification. It cultivates patience, encourages deeper conversations, and allows both individuals to witness one another's true character without the distortions of premature physical or emotional attachment.

A Form of Protection

What we love, we naturally protect. Just as we safeguard our dreams and goals, we must also protect our hearts. When appropriately executed, courting acts as a safeguard against the pain and confusion common in modern dating culture. It sets clear expectations and boundaries, ensuring that both parties are aligned long before deep emotional investments are made. Instead of risking heartbreak through trial and error, courtship offers a structured path for carefully evaluating compatibility, shared values, and long-term potential.

Benefits of a Courtship Approach

When done correctly, the guidelines of courtship help both parties recognize what is truly important before strong feelings or intimate attachments develop. This process prevents premature, impulsive decisions that might otherwise lead to later conflict or heartache. By taking intentional steps to know oneself and one's potential partner, you foster deeper connections built on trust, mutual respect, and a shared vision for the future—rather than on transient, superficial desires.

Consider the following benefits of choosing courtship:

You Save Time:

Some people spend one, five, or even ten years with someone only to discover later that they were not truly compatible. Life is fleeting—who has time to waste on relationships that are not meant to be?

You Save Money:

In many casual relationships, money is spent on each other with little long-term goal in mind, often affecting credit scores and future financial plans. In courtship, expenses are managed more judiciously, ensuring that financial resources are not squandered on transient connections.

No Hard Feelings if It Doesn't Work Out:

Unlike typical breakups, courtship usually involves minimal superficial exchanges. While feelings may develop, they rarely reach a level of dependency that results in emotional devastation if the relationship ends.

A Clear Goal:

When courtship is conducted properly, the objective is clear: it is a pathway toward marriage. Both parties should see enough of the essential fundamentals early on to decide whether to move forward or not. There is no room for indecisiveness, endless "special friend" arrangements, or prolonged periods of uncertainty.

Self-Discovery:

"Know thyself" is an age-old adage for a reason. Courtship

provides the space to reflect on your values and identity—allowing you to truly understand who you are without drifting in and out of relationships for years.

Defined Boundaries and Intentions:

Courtship carries a clear goal with no indecisiveness. It's either moving forward with God's blessings together or respectfully parting ways. There's no time for ambiguous arrangements or prolonged hesitation.

Increased Chances for a Successful Marriage and Family:

Eliminating surprises and addressing core issues before marriage is crucial for building a strong foundation. When both parties understand each other's core beliefs and values and have the support of a like-minded community, the likelihood of a successful, enduring marriage increases.

Divine Guidance:

Ultimately, courtship is from God. Whether you call Him Jehovah, Allah, Christ, Lord, Buddha, Father, or Higher Power, there is a shared understanding that our design—our body, mind, and spirit—is divinely crafted. It is only fitting that we follow a divinely inspired process to honor and maximize that design.

In Summary

The "why" of courtship is ultimately about aligning your life with your highest values. It is about protecting your heart, saving time and resources, and building a solid foundation for a marriage that is as enduring as it is fulfilling. When you engage in courtship, you are not merely looking for a partner—you are preparing yourself for a lifelong journey of growth, love, and mutual respect. You set a standard from the beginning, ensuring that both parties are fully aware of the expectations and the vision for a shared future. This deliberate process lays the groundwork for a successful marriage and a nurturing family environment where both individuals can thrive together with confidence and purpose.

CHAPTER NINE

THE NEED TO KNOW. COURTSHIP QUESTIONS

One of the key components of a successful marriage is eliminating surprises. The more you know about each other and your respective ways, the less likely you are to be caught off guard when life throws unexpected challenges your way. By delving deeply into each other's perspectives, habits, and values before marriage, you create a foundation of trust and security that allows both partners to navigate life's uncertainties with confidence rather than anxiety. Surprises, especially those involving fundamental differences in values, expectations, or lifestyle choices, can place undue stress on a relationship. Taking the time to explore these aspects thoroughly means you build a partnership grounded in awareness and honesty rather than assumptions or hidden truths.

These courtship questions are not always easy; they can become touchy and deeply personal. Yet, it is through these thought-provoking, sometimes difficult conversations that the true depth of compatibility is revealed. When you discuss topics such as finances, faith, family dynamics, personal goals, conflict resolution, and emotional needs, you gain a clearer understanding not only of where you align but also of where differences may exist. Each moment of transparency is a testament to the willingness to engage in meaningful dialogue and to work together toward a shared understanding rather than simply avoiding tough topics. The way each person responds to these challenging questions often serves as a strong indicator of emotional maturity and long-term commitment.

Patience and a solution-oriented mindset are essential during these conversations. A relationship built to last requires both partners to approach challenges with a focus on growth and resolution rather than on conflict or division. Patience creates an environment where each person feels safe to express their thoughts and feelings without fear of judgment while being solution-oriented, which transforms potential obstacles into opportunities for mutual understanding and compromise. This process of navigating difficult conversations with grace and wisdom ultimately shapes the foundation of a resilient and harmonious marriage.

It is also crucial to know what you can handle and what you cannot—and to have the courage to stand by those boundaries. Self-awareness is key when entering a lifelong commitment. Understanding your personal boundaries, core beliefs, and non-negotiables is essential before making a decision as significant as marriage. While love and compromise are vital, so too is recognizing your own limitations and being clear about what you are willing or unwilling to accept in a partnership. Having the strength to acknowledge and communicate these boundaries ensures that both partners enter the relationship with clarity and honesty rather than with unrealistic expectations or suppressed concerns. True strength lies in standing firm on what truly matters while remaining open to growth and adaptation where flexibility is needed.

When both individuals approach their relationship with such intentional awareness, they set the stage for a marriage that is not only enduring but also deeply fulfilling. In the end, these courtship questions are more than just inquiries—they are the building blocks of a relationship grounded in trust, mutual respect, and a shared vision for the future. They ensure that by the time you commit, you have a full understanding of each other's dreams, fears, and values, paving the way for a partnership that can weather the storms and celebrate the triumphs of life together.

Childhood

Our parents, our families, and our upbringing are foundational in shaping who we are and the character we develop. These questions can be sensitive and may evoke a wide range of emotions, so approach them with mental preparedness, transparency, and a heart of healing. Have mercy for yourself and others as you explore these topics.

What was your relationship like with your parent(s)?

Reflect on the dynamics of your upbringing. What aspects do you cherish, and what might you have wished were different? How might these experiences influence the way you choose to raise your own children?

How did your parents handle conflicts or disagreements?

Consider how disagreements were resolved in your home, including interactions among siblings. What conflict resolution strategies were modeled, and how have they shaped your own approach to resolving differences?

If you have siblings, what was your relationship like with them?

Identify the best and the worst qualities you observed in each sibling. How did you overcome any negative traits while still showing them love? What lessons did you learn from these relationships?

How did your family celebrate holidays or special occasions?

Was your celebration characterized by large gatherings or more intimate settings? How did these traditions create a sense of belonging and influence your view of family unity?

Were there specific family traditions that were important to your upbringing?

Reflect on the rituals, stories, or customs that were passed down. How have they contributed to your identity and the values you hold dear?

What kind of neighborhood or community did you grow up in?

Describe the environment—the good, the bad, and the ugly—and explore how this setting helped shape who you are today. In what ways did your community impact your values and perspectives?

How strict, lenient, or balanced were your parents when it came to discipline?

Consider what style of parenting resonated with you and how you might adapt or evolve that approach as your children grow into teenagers. What lessons on discipline and structure did you take from your own experience?

What role did religion or spirituality play in your upbringing?

Was it a guiding force, or did it feel overbearing as a child? Now that you are older, what benefits or insights do you see from your religious or spiritual background, and how might that influence your own parenting style?

How did your parents handle finances?

Reflect on whether their approach to money management

has been passed down to you. What aspects would you keep, and what would you improve upon in managing family finances and planning for the future?

What values were most emphasized in your household?

Think about the importance placed on education, hard work, honesty, or other core principles. How did these values shape your expectations for yourself and others?

Did you feel emotionally supported by your parents or guardians?

If so, in what ways? If not, how would you work to create an environment of emotional support for your own family when it comes time to parent?

How did your family express love or affection?

Reflect on the ways in which love was communicated. If you experienced a lack or faced challenges in this area, how have you healed from it, and how might that inform the way you express love in your future relationships?

Were open conversations about emotions and feelings encouraged in your home?

Consider the communication style within your family. Did

you feel safe sharing your inner thoughts, and how does that impact your approach to intimacy and openness in relationships?

How did your family handle challenges or crises?

What strategies or attitudes were modeled during difficult times? How did these experiences shape your resilience and approach to problem-solving in your own life?

Did your family place importance on culture, family history, or traditions?

Reflect on the significance of cultural heritage and historical narratives in your upbringing. How did these aspects contribute to your identity and your sense of belonging?

What role did friends and extended family play in your upbringing?

Consider the influence of these relationships and how they complemented the immediate family dynamics. How might these broader connections inform the way you build your own support network?

Were there any cultural expectations placed on you while growing up?

How did these expectations influence your behavior, choices, and identity? What lessons can you take from this to empower yourself and your future family?

What was your experience like in school, and did your parents support your education?

Reflect on how your academic journey was shaped by your family's support. Have you continued learning outside traditional education, and how do these experiences inform your values and goals?

Did you get to know your grandparents?

If so, what lessons or wisdom did you gain from them? How have their stories or guidance impacted the person you are today?

What were your family's views on success and failure?

How did they handle both triumphs and setbacks? Consider how these attitudes influenced your own definition of success and the strategies you might adopt when faced with challenges.

By exploring these questions, you can gain invaluable insights into how your childhood experiences have shaped your character, values, and approach to relationships. These reflections serve as a foundation for self-awareness and growth, ensuring that when you step into a partnership, you do so with clarity and a deep understanding of who you are and what you need.

Money, Money, Money

Money is an essential part of our society; without it, living peacefully can be a constant struggle. Even if you aren't super wealthy, the amount of money you have typically fluctuates over time. Our ability to earn and then manage money wisely is crucial. Whether you work a 9-to-5 or are self-employed, having the drive to generate income and the discipline to use it effectively is more important than ever. Since money is so closely tied to security, it becomes an unavoidable topic during courtship. Discussions about money are also intertwined with how we manage debt—a subject that can significantly affect a marriage. The ideal outcome is to have a well-thought-out plan that leads to financial freedom rather than lingering under the burden of debt. And then there's the major financial decision of purchasing a home.

Given today's high interest rates, approaching homeownership should be viewed as an investment rather than simply a place to live until retirement. With mortgage terms of 15, 20, or 30 years, compounded interest can mean that you pay far more than the original price over time— sometimes even carrying the mortgage into old age. I encourage both sides of a courtship to study different strategies for home buying with investments in mind. Don't fall in love with a property to the point where you become locked in financially. Ideally, you want to eventually own your home free and clear so that you can truly enjoy life without the weight of an overwhelming mortgage.

Money Questions

1. How does your monthly budget look?

What are your sources of income and your fixed and variable expenses? How do you balance the two?

2. Do you consider yourself more of a spender or a saver?

Do you plan your spending and saving, or is it more ad hoc? How do you ensure that your financial choices align with your long-term goals?

3. How do you prioritize needs versus wants when spending?

What criteria do you use to decide on expenditures, and how do you maintain that balance?

4. What are your thoughts on credit cards, interest, and debt?

How do you manage credit, and what strategies have you found effective for handling debt?

5. Are there any expenses you consider non-negotiable or essential?

Which ependitures are indispensable to your lifestyle and security, and why?

6. Do you have short-term or long-term financial goals?

What are they, and how can we support each other in reaching these goals?

7. God willing, will we have a retirement savings plan in place as we get older?

How would you feel about having a robust savings account versus just scraping by?

8. If we have children, do you plan on financially supporting their education?

What strategies should we implement to ensure our children receive a good education without jeopardizing our financial stability?

9. What are your thoughts about combining finances after marriage?

Would you prefer a joint, separate, or hybrid approach? Should our accounts be completely transparent, or is some degree of privacy necessary?

10. If we needed to temporarily share a budget to accomplish a goal, would you be willing to participate?

How do you view financial collaboration in achieving common objectives?

11. If a friend or family member needed financial help, would you be comfortable discussing it together first?

How would you handle it if this request came from your personal spending funds?

12. How do you approach holidays and vacations?

Do you plan for them and set aside money in advance, or handle them on a case-by-case basis? Which holidays do you celebrate, and how often do you take vacations?

13. Do you have any money habits you're trying to improve or change?

What are these habits, and what steps are you taking to refine your financial management?

14. Financial disagreements will arise—how do you handle these?

Do you rely on who seems to know best, or are you open to exploring different strategies together? Would you prefer to resolve them privately?

15. If your spending negatively affects our long-term financial stability, how would you feel if I tried to change that behavior?

What measures would you be willing to adopt to ensure our financial health remains intact?

16. Do you have any outstanding debts—such as school loans, credit cards, or personal loans?

If so, what is the total amount, and are you consistently paying them on time? What are the interest rates like?

17. Do you participate in online sports betting or similar activities?

If so, how much do you typically spend in a month, and how would you feel if I disagreed with this habit? Do you spend money on game apps, and if so, how much?

18. Have you always worked a 9-to-5 job, or have you experienced long periods of unemployment?

How much do you make per hour, and are you satisfied with your current career trajectory? Do you plan on moving up within your company, or are you content where you are?

19. How do you feel about me earning my own income through non-traditional means?

Would you support alternative career paths if they align with our values and financial goals?

20. If I had a goal of owning my own business, how would you support that without compromising my plan?

What kind of role do you envision playing in helping me achieve this dream?

21. For how long would you be willing to support my goal of owning a business if you disagreed with the specifics of my plan?

How flexible are you when it comes to supporting entrepreneurial ventures?

22. If my business fails multiple times, how would you continue to support future endeavors?

What are your thoughts on resilience and learning from failure?

23. If I lose my job tomorrow for reasons beyond my control, how would you naturally respond?

What contingency plans do you think we should have in place?

24. If my income alone could cover all our bills, how would you feel about being a "Home Boss Wife"—running a home-based business while managing household responsibilities?

How do you view the balance between traditional roles and modern independence?

25. Some couples have the best of everything—homes, cars, clothes—but must work long hours to sustain that lifestyle.

If this lifestyle starts to erode family time and mental well-being, would you feel comfortable downgrading some of these luxuries, or would you suggest a different solution to maintain balance?

26. Have you ever had your own business?

If so, what was it, and is it still running? What did you learn about yourself in that process?

27. What are your thoughts on banks?

How do you view the role of banks in your financial life, and what experiences have shaped that perspective?

28. Have you ever been scammed by a so-called friend or family member?

How did you handle the situation, and what lessons did you learn about trust and financial management?

29. Was the presence—or absence—of money a significant issue in your family growing up?

How did it influence your views on money, and how do you plan to approach financial matters in your own family?

Health Is Wealth

Waking up feeling good is a true blessing in life. When it comes to health—and its many categories—there's simply no price tag on well-being. We talk about Physical Health, Mental Health, and Spiritual Health, all of which contribute to the overall quality of life. At the root of all these is the concept of healing. Nobody in their right mind walks around proclaiming, "I love being sick, I love feeling depressed, or I love eating something only to feel sluggish and get migraines." In a relationship, both parties striving to be healthy in every phase of life is an enormous asset and ultimately a major positive for the marriage.

Let's Define "Heal"

Heal: To make free from injury or disease; to make sound or whole. To restore health and well-being.

It is critical that both individuals are on a path of healing from past relationships and the wounds of childhood before stepping into a new relationship. There are many ways to heal, and it's only fair that we enter a courtship with as few emotional bags as possible. One effective way to begin the healing process is to answer these questions for yourself. Dig deep into your own answers—ask yourself where, why, how, and when these pains originated and what you plan to do about them. Reflect on where you can find help and guidance. Then, when you enter a courtship, you can honestly share, "This is what happened to me, and here is what I'm doing to heal."

The courtship process isn't meant to uncover every deep-rooted pain we carry, but it does provide a framework for addressing issues with mercy and a solution-oriented mindset. These questions, God willing, will help us gain a better understanding of ourselves and each other. By doing so, we prepare to handle the inevitable trials of marriage with care and compassion. In a world where physical, mental, and spiritual abuse can trace their roots all the way from childhood to adulthood, approaching these topics openly is essential.

Questions on Health

General Health and Lifestyle

1. Are you open to discussing our physical, mental, and spiritual health at this time?

If not, can we agree to table the conversation until a mutually appropriate time?

2. Do you have any harmful conditions or bad habits that might cause you or us pain or loss in the long run— or even right now?

3. What are your thoughts on the health insurance industry?

How do you feel about the coverage, its benefits, or limitations?

4. Have you had to use health insurance before?

What was your experience like with the system?

5. Have you had to visit a hospital before for any reason?

What did you learn from those experiences?

6. If you were in charge of the healthcare industry, how would you improve it for everyone?

7. If you don't have health insurance, are you taking any preemptive measures to prepare for emergencies?

8. How important is eating healthy to you?

9. How often do you eat out?

What influences your choices between home-cooked meals and dining out?

10. Where do you usually grocery shop?

Does your shopping reflect a commitment to healthy eating?

11. How important is a home-cooked meal to you?

12. How often do you crave or require a home-cooked meal?

13. How do you feel about eating leftovers on the 2nd or

3rd day?

14. Is it necessary for me, as your partner, to prepare your meals?

15. Was there a strong emphasis on healthy eating during your upbringing?

16. If your eating habits were tasty but not necessarily the healthiest, would you be willing to change or improve them?

17. How do you feel about exercising—such as walking, home workouts, gym sessions, or bike riding?

How frequently do you work out?

18. Do you have any concerns about fertility or reproductive health?

19. How do you feel about vaccinations?

Did you take the COVID vaccine? If we were to have children, what are your thoughts on vaccinating them throughout childhood?

20. Do you get enough sleep?

How many hours of sleep do you typically get?

21. How important is a good bed when it comes to sleep?

22. Did you have good sleep habits while growing up?

23. How much would you invest in a high-quality bed?

24. Have you ever struggled with any form of substance abuse in the past?

25. Do you smoke, drink alcohol, or use recreational drugs?

If so, how often? At what point does usage shift from recreational to abuse?

26. If an addiction were to develop, would you seek help or insist you're in control?

27. How would you handle the emergence of a new addiction after marriage—especially if it wasn't apparent during courtship?

28. How do you manage stress, anxiety, and depression?

29. Have you ever taken medication for mental health challenges?

30. How do you handle physical pain?

Do you see a doctor immediately, try home remedies, or self-medicate?

31. What are your thoughts on fasting?

32. Would you be willing to try it?

33. Do you have specific food preferences or aversions?

34. Do you regularly take any medications or supplements?

35. Are you aware of any generational medical conditions in your family?

36. How often do you get health check-ups and screenings?

37. Do you have any allergies?

Do you have any chronic health conditions, and what measures are you taking to manage them?

Sensitive Topics on Past Trauma and Abuse

(Please ensure that both you and your courtmate are ready to address these sensitive questions before asking.)

1. Did you grow up witnessing physical abuse in your household?

2. If so, what were the causes of the abuse?

3. What actions were taken to stop the abuse?

4. Do you think witnessing it still affects you subconsciously?

5. Were you personally subjected to physical or mental abuse while growing up?

6. Do you believe you have been healed from that past abuse?

7. If not, how do you feel about working on healing further?

8. As a teen and as an adult, have you been in any abusive relationships?

If so, how many, and how did you transition from one to another?

9. Did you exhibit any abusive tendencies during your youth or adulthood?

10. If so, what are you doing to overcome those behaviors?

11. When upset or in disagreement, do you tend to curse or call others derogatory names?

12. How frequently do you use such language?

13. Do you have moments of rapid emotional shifts—calm one minute, then extremely angry the next?

14. Do you believe that cheating or physical abuse are justifiable grounds for divorce?

15. While growing up, have you ever experienced sexual abuse by family, friends, or partners?

16. Have you sought help or addressed that pain?

17. If not, would you be willing to try various forms of help and healing?

18. If these painful experiences reemerge in our marriage, what solutions would you propose?

19. Do you still see any individuals who contributed to these negative experiences on a regular basis?

20. If we were to have children, how would you protect them from any form of abuse?

Social Life

Our social lives are an important aspect of who we are and how we connect with the world around us. Through these questions, we invite honest reflections on what fun, connection, and balance mean to you and how we can nurture a healthy social life together.

1. What is the meaning of "fun" to you, and how can we ensure we have fun together?

Consider what activities or experiences light you up and how we can share those moments to build joyful memories as a couple.

2. Are there any activities or environments that you consciously avoid when it comes to having fun?

Reflect on any situations that make you uncomfortable or trigger negative feelings so we can be mindful in our social planning.

3. How do you feel about your partner spending time with single friends of the same gender?

Think about the balance between independence and togetherness, and how trust and transparency can guide these social interactions.

4. What is your ideal balance of time between family/children, friends, and just the two of us?

Define what a harmonious mix looks like for you and how we can plan our schedules to honor each of these relationships.

5. In the future, when married, how would you feel about your partner having a curfew?

Explore your expectations around personal freedom, mutual respect, and safety within the context of our shared life.

6. How do you handle disagreements with friends, social groups, or your spiritual house of worship?

Share your strategies for conflict resolution and how you navigate differences within your broader social circles.

7. How often would you like to go on chaperoned dates before marriage?

Consider the role of structured social interactions in building a strong foundation and what frequency feels appropriate for you.

8. How involved do you want to be in your partner's social circle?

Reflect on whether you prefer to integrate deeply with each other's friends and community or maintain some separate spaces.

9. Do you enjoy meeting new people, or do you prefer a close-knit group?

Think about your social preferences and how they contribute to your sense of security and fulfillment.

10. How do you feel about joining groups, clubs, or community organizations?

Discuss whether participation in organized activities is a priority for you and how it might enrich our lives.

11. How often do you like to travel in a year, and what modes of travel do you prefer (driving, planes, or

boats)?

Consider your passion for exploration and adventure and how travel fits into your overall lifestyle.

12. Are you comfortable spending time apart to pursue individual social activities?

Reflect on the importance of personal space and how it complements the time we share as a couple.

13. In a typical week, how often do you prefer going out for walks, visiting parks, or enjoying the outdoors compared to staying in?

Define your ideal balance between outdoor activities and home-based relaxation.

14. How do you feel about hosting friends and family events at home?

Share your thoughts on being a gracious host and creating a welcoming environment for those we care about.

15. How important is it for you to socialize with your partner's family during events and holidays?

Reflect on the role extended family plays in your life and

how you envision nurturing these relationships.

16. What does an ideal weekend look like for you, and how do you prefer to spend your downtime?

Describe your perfect weekend, whether it's filled with quiet moments, lively gatherings, or a mix of both.

17. How many hours a day do you typically spend on your phone or laptop?

Consider whether your screen time supports or detracts from your quality of life and personal interactions.

18. How much of that time is spent scrolling through social media platforms like TikTok, Facebook, or YouTube?

Reflect on the impact of digital distractions on your well-being and social engagement.

19. After marriage, how would you feel about both partners having full access to each other's phones and electronic devices?

Discuss your views on digital transparency versus privacy and how you might establish healthy boundaries.

20. How do you feel about your partner having social media accounts that share personal life details?

Explore the balance between sharing and privacy in an age of constant connectivity.

21. If your future partner wanted you to remove "eye-catching" pre-marriage pictures posted online, would you be willing to do so?

Consider the significance of preserving the sanctity of your shared life versus maintaining your personal digital history.

22. How would you feel if your partner shared a disagreement, argument, or personal event online about you, friends, or family without naming names?

Reflect on the importance of discretion and respect for personal matters in public forums.

23. What if such sharing occurred after we both agreed not to do it?

Think about trust and the expectations you have regarding honoring mutual agreements about privacy.

24. How often do you take selfies or share updates about new items and vacations online?

Evaluate how social media habits influence your sense of self and your connection with others.

25. How do you feel about having friends who you know are cheating on their partners?

Consider whether and how you'd intervene or offer support in such situations.

26. If you discovered a friend or family member was cheating, would you stay out of it, offer help, or try to intervene personally?

Discuss your values regarding loyalty, honesty, and the importance of protecting those you care about.

27. If we are part of a spiritual community, how would you feel about your partner breaking some of the community's foundational rules?

Reflect on the balance between personal freedom and communal expectations and how these values impact your relationship.

Believer and Knower

1. Do you believe in a Higher Power (God)?

If so, how do you define God in your life? Consider how your understanding of a Higher Power shapes your daily actions and decisions.

2. How important is your faith or spiritual walk in your daily life?

Reflect on whether your spirituality influences your routines, decisions, and interactions.

3. To what degree would you say you actually follow the principles of your belief?

Evaluate how consistently your actions align with your spiritual values and teachings.

4. Do you follow a particular religion or spiritual path?

Describe the specific traditions or practices that guide your life and how they impact your worldview.

5. How do you handle doubts or questions about your faith?

Consider whether you seek answers through study, prayer,

or discussions with mentors and how this process influences your spiritual growth.

6. How do you handle it when your partner doubts God or questions the spiritual standards expected of men and women?

Reflect on how you would support your partner through moments of spiritual uncertainty while maintaining your own convictions.

7. How do you feel about giving charity in monetary forms?

What role does generosity play in your life, and how do you balance giving with your financial responsibilities?

8. How do you feel about engaging in charity work for those with less?

Explore the ways in which active service and volunteering might align with your values.

9. Have you ever donated or given to a homeless person?

Reflect on your experiences with direct acts of kindness and what they taught you about compassion.

10. Have you ever talked to and encouraged a homeless person?

Consider the impact of personal outreach on your spiritual and emotional well-being.

11. In a typical month, how often would you say you attend a service?

Think about how regular participation in communal worship shapes your sense of community and spiritual growth.

12. How often do you pray or meditate?

Describe the role of personal prayer or meditation in your daily routine and its effect on your inner peace.

13. Do you pray verbally only, or do you incorporate motion and body movements into your prayer?

Reflect on the physical expressions of your faith and how they enhance your spiritual connection.

14. Are there any rituals, holidays, or traditions that are important for you to observe or participate in?

Consider the role these practices play in grounding your beliefs and connecting you to your community.

15. Do you expect me to participate in your personal or our shared religious or spiritual practices?

Discuss how you envision faith playing a role in our relationship and what level of involvement is important to you.

16. How do you feel about marrying someone with different beliefs?

Explore the potential challenges and opportunities that interfaith relationships might present.

17. How would you feel about our children—or your future children—marrying someone with a different spiritual walk or belief?

Reflect on how you would approach the transmission of faith and values to the next generation.

18. Would you be comfortable attending a spiritual event that is different from your own?

Consider your openness to experiencing diverse spiritual expressions and learning from them.

19. How would you handle disagreements between each other within your agreed faith?

Discuss strategies for resolving conflicts while honoring shared religious values.

20. How important is it that we share the same religious views?

Reflect on the role that religious alignment plays in long-term compatibility and relationship satisfaction.

21. How much does your faith influence your moral and ethical decisions?

Describe the connection between your spiritual beliefs and the choices you make in everyday life.

22. If you could make an extra $10k on a business deal that only you and God know about, but it required going against a part of your beliefs, would you still do it?

Consider how you balance financial gain with moral integrity and what sacrifices you are willing to make for your faith.

23. What if your partner did it?

Reflect on how you would navigate a situation where your partner's actions conflicted with your shared values.

24. How does your faith interact with how you handle stress, grief, or hardship?

Describe the coping mechanisms inspired by your spiritual beliefs during challenging times.

25. How do you feel about life and death?

Share your perspectives on mortality and what lies beyond, shaped by your faith.

26. How do you handle the loss of close loved ones?

Reflect on your process of grieving and the spiritual or practical support you rely on during times of loss.

27. Do you sometimes blame your faith or God for your losses?

Consider whether you've ever questioned your beliefs during difficult periods and how that has influenced your recovery.

28. While no one can dictate another person's grieving period, what would you do if your grief started turning into depression?

Explore the steps you'd take to help yourself—or your partner—recover and find healing.

29. What type of ceremony or procedures do you envision when your time comes?

Reflect on your preferences for end-of-life rituals and how they align with your spiritual beliefs.

30. How do you feel about seeking advice on major life trials from leaders within our shared faith?

Consider the importance of mentorship and guidance from experienced spiritual leaders.

31. Do you believe in divine intervention or fate?

Share any testimonies or experiences that reinforce your belief in a higher power's influence on your life.

32. If we have children, how much spirituality do you envision instilling in them?

Would you prefer to continue with the same level of spiritual emphasis you experienced growing up or adjust it in any way?

33. Would you be comfortable if your future children explored different faiths?

Reflect on the balance between guiding your children and

allowing them the freedom to choose their own spiritual paths.

34. Have you ever held a leadership role within your faith or spiritual community?

Describe any responsibilities you've had and how they've shaped your understanding of faith.

35. How would you handle it if someone within your faith lied to you or about you?

Discuss the importance of honesty and integrity within your community, as well as your approach to reconciliation.

36. Do you believe there is more after this life?

Share your thoughts on the afterlife and how that belief influences your day-to-day decisions.

Do you believe in Karma?

Reflect on whether the idea of cosmic justice resonates with you and how it might affect your outlook on life.

37. How can we help and nurture each other's spiritual growth during our courtship and marriage?

Explore ways we can encourage one another to deepen our faith, whether through shared practices, open discussions, or mutual support.

38. How often can we pray together?

Define what joint prayer or meditation might look like and how frequently it should occur.

39. Do you stay in touch with and seek advice from the elders in your spiritual community?

Describe how these relationships influence your faith and decision-making.

40. How often do you visit these mentors or elders?

Reflect on the frequency of these interactions and the impact they have on your spiritual life.

41. How far would you go in assisting them if they had a need?

Consider the depth of your commitment to those who have guided you and how that reflects on your personal values.

A House is Not a Home Without…

Creating a true home goes far beyond simply having a roof over your head—it's about cultivating an environment filled with love, understanding, and shared responsibility. As we prepare for a life together, it's important to address how we will manage our household and support each other's roles. Consider the following questions as a guide to establishing a balanced, nurturing home life:

1. Do we both agree that one of us will be a full-time homemaker or do we expect both of us to work outside the home?

Reflect on our individual goals and the lifestyle we envision. What does it mean for each of us to contribute, whether through work in the home or a career outside?

2. If one of us stays home, for how long will it be until the children reach school age or permanently?

Discuss whether this arrangement is viewed as a temporary phase or a long-term commitment and how that might change as circumstances evolve.

3. Who is responsible for cleaning the house, doing laundry, and handling general home maintenance?

Clearly outline expectations for daily tasks and long-term upkeep to ensure a balanced division of labor.

4. Do we view homemaking as a temporary role or a long-term commitment?

Consider whether the role of the homemaker is something that can evolve over time as personal and family needs change.

5. If one of us wants to change roles (for example, the homemaker wants to return to work, or the working partner wants to stay home), how will we handle that transition?

Plan for flexibility by discussing potential transitions and how we might support each other during changes.

6. How often should we check in and re-evaluate our roles and responsibilities as our family grows or as circumstances change?

Establish regular "household meetings" or check-ins to ensure that our arrangement remains fair and meets our evolving needs.

7. If our home dynamic isn't working, how do we

approach conversations about restructuring our responsibilities without resentment or blame?

Develop a conflict-resolution strategy that emphasizes open communication, empathy, and a willingness to adapt.

8. If the homemaker wants to pursue hobbies, further education, or part-time work, how will we support that?

Explore ways to ensure that personal growth and self-care are supported, regardless of the role each partner assumes.

9. How do we feel about the working partner assisting with chores or childcare after work, or should they be considered "off duty" in the evenings?

Discuss expectations around after-work contributions, ensuring that both partners feel valued and that responsibilities are shared equitably.

10. How do we ensure that the homemaker or working partner gets breaks and personal time without feeling guilty?

Consider ideas such as designating a regular "me time" or a special day—like a Mother's/Father's Day once a week or twice a month—devoted solely to self-care and relaxation, free from household duties.

11. What will we do if one partner feels unappreciated or undervalued in their role?

Plan to routinely express gratitude and recognition for each other's contributions, ensuring that both financial and domestic efforts are celebrated.

12. How do we handle decision-making at home?

Determine whether decisions will be made jointly or if one partner will have the final say on certain matters, and set clear guidelines to avoid misunderstandings.

13. How will we ensure that we show appreciation for each other's contributions to the marriage and household?

Discuss regular practices for expressing gratitude—whether through verbal affirmations, thoughtful gestures, or shared activities that honor both roles.

14. If one partner feels overwhelmed in their role—whether homemaking or working—how will we address and redistribute responsibilities?

Agree on strategies for alleviating stress, such as temporary adjustments in duties or seeking external help, to maintain balance and prevent burnout.

15. Do we have different cleanliness standards, and how can we compromise if one of us is tidier than the other?

Share personal standards and negotiate a middle ground that respects both perspectives while maintaining a comfortable living space.

16. Will we designate specific tasks for each person (e.g., one cooks while the other cleans), or will we share all duties equally?

Discuss the advantages and challenges of specialized roles versus a shared approach, and decide what works best for our partnership.

17. How do we feel about outsourcing tasks like deep cleaning, lawn care, or home repairs if we can afford it?

Evaluate whether hiring outside help might improve our quality of life and reduce stress and under what conditions it would be a beneficial option.

18. How do we divide household responsibilities such as cooking, cleaning, and laundry?

Consider a detailed plan or schedule that clearly outlines each partner's responsibilities, ensuring fairness and transparency.

19. What are your expectations for balancing household duties if both of us work?

Discuss realistic expectations and potential adjustments, such as flexible work hours or shared responsibilities, to ensure the home runs smoothly.

20. If one of us is a homemaker, how do we ensure that this role is valued equally to financial contributions?

Affirm that every role is vital to the household's well-being. Discuss ways to recognize and honor the work done at home, making sure it receives the same respect as external contributions.

Communication is Key

Effective communication forms the backbone of any strong relationship. By engaging in open and honest dialogue, we build trust, resolve conflicts, and deepen our connection. Consider the following questions to help us understand and improve the way we interact with each other:

1. How would you describe your communication style?

Are you more direct or indirect? Do you tend to be emotional, logical, or a mix of both? Reflect on how your style influences conversations.

2. What are your strengths and weaknesses in communication?

Recognize the areas where you excel and those where you'd like to grow so we can support each other's development.

3. How do you prefer to receive constructive criticism?

Discuss whether you appreciate gentle feedback, direct comments, or a different approach entirely.

4. How do you feel about using technology (text, email, calls) for important conversations?

Consider when technology is helpful and when face-to-face discussion might be more appropriate.

5. Do you feel comfortable expressing your emotions openly with me? Why or why not?

Share your comfort level and any factors that may encourage or inhibit open emotional expression.

6. How do you typically respond when you're feeling overwhelmed or stressed?

Explore your coping mechanisms and how they affect our interactions.

7. How do you usually handle conflict?

Do you prefer discussing issues immediately, taking time apart, or using another method to resolve disagreements?

8. What are some past conflicts you've experienced in relationships, and how do you think you handled them?

Reflect on lessons learned and consider ways to improve future conflict resolution.

9. If there is a need to apologize, what would you do to

show it's sincere?

Share your approach to making amends and restoring trust after a disagreement.

10. How do you feel about apologizing—do you find it easy or difficult?

Understanding this can help us navigate challenging moments with empathy.

11. What is the best way for me to approach you when you're feeling hurt or upset?

Discuss the methods that help you feel safe and understood during sensitive times.

12. How do you react when someone raises their voice during an argument?

Consider whether this escalates conflict for you or prompts you to seek resolution.

13. How can we ensure that we resolve conflicts in a healthy, productive way?

Explore strategies to turn disagreements into opportunities for growth.

14. Do you feel that I listen to you attentively? What could I do better?

Open a dialogue about listening habits and how we can improve mutual understanding.

15. How do you usually show that you're listening to someone?

Reflect on verbal and non-verbal cues that make you feel heard.

16. What makes you feel truly heard and understood in a conversation?

Share specific actions or words that resonate with you.

17. How can we prevent misunderstandings in our daily communication?

Discuss proactive strategies, such as clarifying intentions and summarizing discussions.

18. How should we handle miscommunications when they arise?

Define a process for addressing errors quickly and compassionately.

19. How much time do you think we should spend talking to each other daily?

Establish expectations for regular communication that nurtures our connection.

20. What topics do you find difficult to discuss, and how can I support you in talking about them?

Identify sensitive areas and brainstorm ways to approach these conversations gently.

21. How do you feel about discussing our relationship with close friends or family?

Consider what boundaries feel appropriate when sharing personal matters.

22. How should we handle conversations about finances, parenting, or other major life decisions?

Outline a collaborative approach that respects both partners' perspectives.

23. How do we set boundaries when we need alone time or space to process emotions?

Establish guidelines for personal space while maintaining

connection.

24. How do you prefer to receive love—through words, actions, gifts, or physical touch?

Identify your love language so that we can better support each other's needs.

25. How do you typically express appreciation for the people you love?

Share your methods of showing gratitude and how they make you feel valued.

26. What words or gestures make you feel most appreciated in our relationship?

Define specific actions that reinforce your sense of being cherished.

27. How often do you like to hear words of affirmation from your partner?

Determine the frequency and style of positive reinforcement that resonates with you.

28. How can we improve our communication to make it even stronger?

Brainstorm actionable steps to enhance clarity, empathy, and effectiveness in our exchanges.

29. Are there any past communication habits from previous relationships that you want to avoid in our marriage?

Reflect on lessons learned and identify patterns to consciously leave behind.

30. How should we check in with each other to ensure we're both happy with our communication?

Consider regular check-ins or structured conversations as part of our routine.

31. Are you open to reading books, attending workshops, or seeking counseling to improve our communication over time?

Discuss your willingness to invest in ongoing personal and mutual growth.

Security

A strong sense of security—both physical and emotional—is essential for a thriving relationship. Addressing questions about personal and family safety, emergency preparedness, and financial security can help us create a safe, supportive home environment.

1. **What forms of security do you currently practice?**

Reflect on measures you already have in place for personal and home safety.

2. **How important is security to you?**

Evaluate the role that safety plays in your overall well-being and peace of mind.

3. **Do you own any weapons for self-defense?**

If yes, discuss how often you carry them and the level of comfort you have with them.

4. **Have you received any training on handling your weapon?**

Consider the importance of proper training for responsible ownership.

5. **Are there other ways you feel secure without the**

need for a weapon?

Explore alternative security measures that may align more closely with your values.

6. How would you feel if I preferred not to have a weapon in our home?

Discuss how differing views on self-defense might be reconciled.

7. How do you handle emergency situations, such as break-ins or natural disasters?

Share any experiences or plans you have for dealing with unexpected events.

8. Do you believe in having a home security system, and would you be open to investing in one?

Discuss the role of technology and professional systems in our overall safety plan.

9. Are you comfortable with self-defense training, and would you consider taking a class together?

Explore options for enhancing our security skills as a couple.

10. How do you feel about discussing a safety plan for our home and family?

Consider the importance of proactive planning and how it can be integrated into our lifestyle.

11. Do you believe in keeping emergency supplies (food, water, medical kits) in case of unexpected situations?

Evaluate our preparedness for emergencies and any potential improvements.

12. How do you protect personal information and sensitive data from identity theft or cyber threats?

Reflect on strategies for maintaining digital security in an increasingly connected world.

13. Are you open to having surveillance cameras or smart locks installed in our home for added security?

Discuss the balance between privacy and safety measures.

14. How do you feel about involving neighbors or a community watch program in ensuring neighborhood safety?

Consider how community involvement can enhance our

collective security.

15. Have you ever experienced a security threat or dangerous situation, and how did you handle it?

Share past experiences to better understand your approach to safety.

16. How would you respond if we faced a safety concern while traveling together?

Discuss your instincts and strategies for maintaining security on the road or in unfamiliar environments.

17. What are your thoughts on teaching our future children about personal safety and emergency preparedness?

Explore the importance of instilling these values from a young age.

18. Do you think it's important to have a financial security plan in place (such as insurance or savings) in case of unforeseen events?

Reflect on the role of financial preparedness in overall security.

Scenario

It's late at night, and you are both in bed when you suddenly hear a noise downstairs. What would you do as a Man and as a Woman?

Consider how your roles and instincts might guide your immediate response, ensuring both safety and clear communication between you during a potential crisis.

Affirm that every role is vital to the household's well-being. Discuss ways to recognize and honor the work done at home, making sure it receives the same respect as external contributions.

Closing Remarks

Thank you for your support of this book and this movement. I wrote this book with our youth in mind, and over time it has grown to speak to adults as well. In a world where the erosion of family values and strong relationships is increasingly evident, The Noble Courtship stands as a beacon of hope—a call to restore the foundational love that strengthens us, our children, and our communities.

This book is more than just words on a page; it is a call to action and a guide to rediscovering the core values that form the bedrock of lasting relationships and resilient families. In a society where commitment often feels fleeting, and the sanctity of love is overshadowed by convenience and superficiality, it is essential that we return to the timeless principles of trust, respect, and devotion. True love requires effort, patience, and an unwavering dedication to growth— both as individuals and as partners.

Embrace the process of courtship. Grow, learn, and transform yourself so that you can qualify for that special one that God has destined for you. This journey is not just about finding love; it is about becoming the kind of person who is ready to give and receive love in its fullest expression.

It is about preparing your heart, mind, and spirit to build a relationship that endures—a relationship that not only enriches your own life but also creates a ripple effect, strengthening families, communities, and future generations.

May this book inspire you to seek love with purpose and to cherish the beauty of a courtship rooted in faith and integrity. May you never settle for anything less than the profound, unwavering love that God intends for you. Thank you for joining me on this journey, for believing in the power of love, and for choosing to walk the noble path toward a relationship that is both meaningful and enduring.